Golf with a View

1895   1995

BROADWAY GOLF CLUB

Dr. C. T. Standring, Founder

Golf with a View

Broadway Golf Club 1895–1995

by

Patricia Penny

To Audrey – Best Wishes

Pat x

Grant and Hobbs, Worcestershire 1996

ISBN 0 907186 85 8

Set in 11 on 13 point New Baskerville
Typeset and printed in Great Britain by
Severnside Printers Limited
Upton-upon-Severn, Worcestershire, England

Published by Grant and Hobbs
The Coach House, Cutnall Green,
Droitwich, Worcestershire WR9 0PQ

Golf with a View

Broadway Golf Club 1895–1995

Published in a limited edition of 1000 copies

Copy No:

Patricia Penny

Contents

Acknowledgements

When I was first asked by a member of the newly formed Centenary Committee to write this history I felt surprised and possibly flattered. My only experience of writing had been of various academic treatises and 20 odd years "at the chalk face" trying to persuade others to write! I decided to agree to the suggestion, in spite of some misgivings, not being one of the longer-standing members of the club, but perhaps this was an advantage as I had no preformed opinions to influence me.

It was immediately apparent that it was more than a one-person task, especially when the first thing we discovered was that the long-accepted founding date of 1896 was at least one year out. Fortunately my husband shared my interest in social history and I was able to enlist his help in research and call on his 30 years of golfing experience. In fact it has really been a joint venture.

We used different kinds of source material – written, photographic and reminiscent. Sometimes what was recalled did not match written records; we decided the latter would be the more accurate, being contemporary.

It is impossible in a work of this nature to mention everyone and we apologise if anyone feels neglected but we have done our best with what turned out to be a gargantuan task.

I would like to extend my grateful thanks to all those who have contributed information and source material for the book.

PERSONAL REMINISCENCES

Les Arnold, a man of over 80, who took the time to write out at some length not only his personal memories of people long gone but, as our longest serving member, what he recalled of the running of the club.

Jack Gorin, also over 80, for the loan of his photographs and for spending an afternoon with a tape recorder describing the course in his early years as a member and the building of the new nine.

Keith Gilbert, whose close association with the running of the club over many years, made him the person to read the rough draft of this history.

Frank Stewart, P. O. Heatherley, Les Yardley, three venerable gentlemen, for their recollections.

Frank Tams for information regarding the junior section, Ken Marshall, the senior section.

Finally the many other people who have shown interest and given information.

OTHER SOURCES

Mrs. Christine Pemberton for loan of the personal memoirs of her late husband, Mr. Guy Pemberton (this opened the door to the early years).
Mrs. Sabin, Lighthorne, Warwickshire, grandaughter of Dr. Alexander, for loan of family albums.
Lord Neidpath for access to the archives of Stanway Hall.
Peter Lewis, Museum Director, British Golf Museum, St. Andrews.

PHOTOGRAPHY

Mr. D. Jelfs, High Street, Broadway, who has spent hours producing copies of old photographs and illustrations for inclusion.
Mr. Ian Cameron of the *Evesham Journal*, for photography of the course one fine autumn morning and reproduction of some early *Evesham Journal* photographs.
My husband for colour photography.

OTHER CLUB HISTORIANS

Tony Gattrill, Cirencester; John Gee, Stratford-on-Avon; David Cadney, Olton; Michael Robinson, Burhill.

PRIMARY SOURCES

The minutes and files of Broadway Golf Club, 1901 to present date.

PRESS AND OTHER PUBLICATIONS

History of Broadway,
  Dr. C. C. Houghton.
Golf Annual, 1897.
Victoria County History of
  Worcestershire.
Golf – A Way of Life,
  edited by Peter Alliss.

Evesham Journal, 1894 onwards.
Gloucester Echo.
Birmingham Post.
Birmingham Gazette.
Daily Mail.
The Birmingham (later *Midland*)
  Golfer, 1911–15.

Patricia Penny

Message from the President

I was born in Weston Subedge and have spent the whole of my life within hailing distance of Broadway Golf Club. I played as a boy of 16 when Broadway was a nine-hole course, beloved by its members but little known and hanging on by a thread. This history does not consist of descriptions of great events or international golfing heroes, but years of struggle to keep afloat and a great deal of hard work by a few dedicated enthusiasts, which makes the present stature of the club all the more remarkable.

I am proud to be the president in this, the club's centenary year and hope that today's members will be able to pass on a similar legacy to the future.

David Robinson
President

From the Centenary Captain

To be captain of a golf club during its centenary year is something very special indeed, and it has been a privilege and an honour for me to have held that position at Broadway.

This book not only records the full history of the club but its final chapter covers the centenary year itself, with details of events held to commemorate this great occasion. I am sure that all our members and their families will find pleasure in this publication and that it will be a treasured keepsake for many years to come.

I must thank David Robinson and his centenary committee for their unstinting efforts in making the year a success, and Pat and Frank Penny for their research and writing of this history. As we go into the next century I know that members and visitors alike will continue to enjoy Broadway Golf Club in its beautiful Cotswold setting.

Charles Pieters
Centenary Captain

Chapter One

Laying the Foundations

G OLF had been played in Scotland since the fifteenth century when King James found it necessary to ban the game because it interfered with archery practice. The game played there was on rough ground with homemade equipment without thought of class distinction. There were no golf clubs, no written rules. Only slight inroads were made in England with the foundation of the Royal Blackheath Golf Club in 1766. In 1818 we have the Old Manchester Club on Kersal Moor. For nearly 50 years these remained the only established clubs in England and then came the nineteenth century explosion! Broadway Golf Club was one of the many.

Growth of Golf Clubs in the UK

1800	1870	1890	1900	1910
7	34	387	2,330	4,150

Growth of Golf Clubs in Worcestershire

1880, Country Club, Malvern.
1890, Redditch (Ipsley) – then in quick succession, Kidderminster, Hagley, Blackwell, Kings Norton, Pershore, Stourbridge, Studley, Robin Hood, Evesham, Broadway, Bromsgrove. Droitwich came next, and finally Worcester City in 1899. Thus it can be seen that during the last 19 years of the nineteenth century, 14 clubs sprang up.

Gloucestershire could boast a mere two clubs in 1890 but by 1900 this number also had increased to 14, although several of the clubs against whom Broadway played in the early days failed to survive: for example Chastleton, Moreton-in-Marsh, Stow-in-the-Wold.

One reason for this increase was the extraordinary advance in the manufacture and design of golf balls from 1848 onwards. It was discovered that the juice of the Malaysian gutta percha tree made good golf balls when allowed to thicken in moulds. Later the modern phenomenon of mass

1

production meant cheaper and readily obtainable balls which was very significant in developing the popularity of the game. Better balls inspired the development of better clubs and players demanded more and better courses.

Alongside this, mention could be made of the changing social attitudes which is significant to Broadway. In the early years in Scotland golf was undoubtedly played by the ordinary folk. But it was not long before merchants and noblemen used their financial advantage to buy the improved equipment and these people eventually wanted to create their own clubs and courses. It was this elitist game which spread over the border to England. By Victorian times the rapid expansion of golf was almost entirely through private clubs to which the local artisans had no access.

HISTORY OF BROADWAY VILLAGE

Did Broadway have this pre-requisite of elite society with the time, money and inclination to form a golf club? At the start of the nineteenth century the answer to this question would possibly have been, "No". However in the middle of the century social change began to take place, brought about by the arrival of the railway to Evesham in 1860.

In the seventeenth century Broadway became important as a major coaching centre when the stage coach was the usual way to travel. The village stood on the main road from London to Worcester, along which seven four-horse coaches passed daily, plus private traffic and heavy goods wagons. All that was demanded to keep this traffic on the move had to be provided. Extra horses had to be found to pull the vehicles up Fish Hill. These were hired out by a haulage business which was located at the end of the village, handily placed opposite a public house (now Halstead House). There were 33 public houses in Broadway catering for overnight stops as well as a community of grooms, ostlers and blacksmiths. In addition there were services which always accompanied a thriving, busy population – a bakehouse (now the Broadway Hotel), mill, forge, saddlers, wheelwrights. Stone farmhouses, barns and cottages straggled up the road at the upper end of the village.

The coming of the railway to Evesham made the stage coach obsolete and, almost overnight, Broadway entered a period of economic decline. However, what on the one hand was a loss, on the other became a gain because the village changed to a quiet, beautiful backwater, soon to be discovered by Victorian artists, writers and wealthy professional and business men. It was they who bought up the property, changing and converting old inns, farms, barns into gentlemen's residences, adding to the stock of very desirable residential properties already in the village. This change in

Broadway, this influx of wealth, made the end of the nineteenth century the right time, the right place with the right people for the foundation of a golf club.

The circumstances had prepared the way; the next ingredient was the arrival of Dr. C. T. Standring.

1894, ARRIVAL OF THE FOUNDER

At first just a name on a photograph in the clubhouse and a signature on old minutes, it has been fascinating to put flesh on the skeleton of this man who, according to his contemporaries, was quite remarkable.

Charles Turner Standring was born in 1865 and was educated at Blackheath School (probably where his interest in golf originated). After various medical experience, he came to Broadway in 1894 at the age of 29, and practised there for 30 years from his house The Laurels, now renamed Broom House. We were lucky enough to be able to borrow the personal memoirs of Mr. Guy Pemberton, from which it was possible to glean many personal details of Dr. Standring. Mr. Pemberton, an architect, was a member of a family who were brass founders in Birmingham. Mr. Pemberton senior and Guy, who was only 11 years old at the time, were among the few founder members of Broadway Golf Club in 1894. He describes Dr. Standring as a devout churchman, a conscientious up-to-date doctor and a keen sportsman. In the first few years he was in the village, he re-organised the cricket club where "He was a fair bat and good fielder" (*Evesham Journal*, obituary); formed the football club; he was secretary of the tennis club and "He played a good game in old-fashioned style". (ibid.) But what is most important, he founded the golf club. "As a golfer Dr. Standring played a game of his own, and in a team was a very useful asset. He was not a long driver but he was a difficult man to beat". (ibid.) Among his other activities were croquet and billiards, still leaving himself time to take part in village entertainments as we are told he had a good tenor voice.

Official Duties

MO to Cirencester Club, Great Western Railway Staff, Post Office Staff.
1914–18 war at Farncombe and Abbey Manor Hospitals.
MO for Belgian refugees.

One can only gasp at the extent of his activities. To quote from Mr. Pemberton, "He had unbounded energy, great organising ability, and a sort of Pied Piper magnetism, which drew everybody, young and old, into his schemes, which were invariably promoted for the good of others. In fact he ran the village".

3

Broadway must have been a very insular community at the end of the nineteenth century. The stage coach had gone, the railway had not yet arrived, and although the motor car had been invented in the early 1890s it was not to come into general use for many years. House parties, soirées and amateur entertainments provided the main points of social contact. Levels of society were clearly defined and everyone moved in their own social circle. When Dr. Standring arrived in 1894 his position in this society as a well-qualified medical man must have made it easy for him to contact many people. He would soon have discovered if he had any kindred spirits keen to start playing golf. One member today, Mr. Frank Stewart, who lived in Broadway in the early 1920s and can remember Dr. Standring, says that as boys they often had to help give him a push start in his model T Ford.

There is no official record of how Dr. Standring introduced Broadway to golf but he must have started soon after taking up residence at The Laurels.

MORE FOUNDER MEMBERS

A. F. de Navarro

A name which can be coupled with Dr. Standring's for long service to the club is that of Mr. A. F. de Navarro, of Basque origin. He was captain in 1924, president in 1930–32 and honorary treasurer for many years. He was a man of wealth and an authority on porcelain. He held high rank in the Catholic Church (Papal Chamberlain and Knight Commander of the Order of St. Gregory). He arrived in Broadway a year before the doctor and bought Court Farm at the end of the village. He was married to the beautiful and famous Shakespearean actress Mary Anderson, and together they made Court Farm a Mecca for artists and musicians of note. Mr. de Navarro was a supporter of Broadway Golf Club until his death in 1932.

Isaac Averill

Unfortunately, if minutes existed before 1901, they have been lost and the fixture card of 1899–1900 is one of the few pieces of written evidence of members and activities. In those early days it was the custom to invite some august personage to become president. His

4

name would lend prestige to the club, regardless of golfing ability (although it must be said that one or two were very able players). The first president, Mr. Isaac Averill LD, JP was the squire of Broadway. He lived at Broad Close, a large house still to be seen along the main street. The only trace found of him was his tomb in the old churchyard, which shows him to have come from a medical family. Whether he had any golfing prowess or not remains unknown.

Lord Lifford

Lord Lifford (an Irish title) lived in Austen House. This is now largely empty and is located past the new church. Still living in part of the house is Dr. C. C. Houghton, the unofficial historian of Broadway, and truly a mine of information. He gave me an interesting anecdote regarding Lady Lifford, unconnected with golf but casting a light on the type of person she was. Each Sunday she emerged from the front door of Austen House to go to church; behind her came the butler carrying her prayer book on a silk cushion!

Lord Lifford was president of the club in 1901.

Lord Elcho

The name of Lord Elcho of Stanway House appears as a vice-president in 1899. He became president in 1902 holding the office until 1908. He was a keen golfer and the minutes show he attended many of the meetings during his terms of office. Lord Elcho, heir to the Earl of Wemyss, was a member of an important aristocratic family with a very large acreage of land in

Lord Elcho. Family group showing the two eldest sons killed in the Great War 1914-18

Scotland as well as in the Cotswolds at Stanway. His eldest son, Hugo Charteris, was also a member of Broadway Golf Club. Sadly Hugo and his younger brother were soon to die, victims of World War I.

Lord Elcho was a golfer of note, holding the club record until ousted by Dr. Standring in 1905 – in the early days of the 1901–10 course his score of 80 was considered a remarkable performance.

On the links. Lord Elcho with friends and caddies

The Right Honorable Arthur Balfour MP

Also on the list of 1899 vice-presidents, friend of Lord and Lady Elcho (an especially good "friend" of Lady Elcho according to Kenneth Young, Arthur Balfour's biographer) he was a frequent visitor to Stanway House. Arthur Balfour was leader of the Conservative party until 1911 and Prime Minister from 1902 to 5. According to Mr. de Navarro in a speech made at Broadway Cricket Club Dinner on March 30th, 1895, Broadway was "the Golf Links famous for Mr. Balfour's baptismal appellative" which in plain English means it was at Broadway "he caught the bug". It was A. J.  Balfour's enthusiasm for the game which prompted many of his fellow politicians to take up the sport in and around London in the latter part of the nineteenth century. To quote Mr. Pemberton again, "I played in a very interesting foursome in the gutty days; I and Lord Elcho against Dr. Oliver Lodge and A. J. Balfour. I remember I won a shilling from him and

6

made some feeble joke about the country affording it as he had just been made Chancellor of the Exchequer". A. J. Balfour remained a paid-up member of the club at least until 1918, and was elected an honorary member in 1922. He definitely played in matches for the club against Evesham; there must be few country golf clubs able to boast of the support of such an important politician.

Birmingham Post, April 15th, 1912, Mr. Balfour at Golf. His Defeat on the Broadway Course.

The Right Hon. A. J. Balfour spent the weekend as the guest of Lord and Lady Elcho at Stanway House.

On Saturday afternoon he took part in a golf match on the links of the Broadway Club, playing for the club against an Evesham team. Broadway were strongly represented, and Mr. Balfour occupied a somewhat lowly position in a team of ten. He, however, found his opponent, Mr. E. W. Beck who was playing quite a strong game, too good for him, and was beaten by 4 up and 3. Mr. Beck was playing a very long game from the tee, and the greens, which were indifferent, bothered Mr. Balfour as they did three weeks ago … The match was halved, each side winning five events.

START OF PLAY

It is from Mr. Pemberton's memoirs we know exactly where and how they played in the earliest days when the club was of a peripatetic nature. "Once again my hero, the dear old Doc. takes me by one hand, pushes a cleek into another, and teaches me the rudiments of the 'Royal and Ancient Game'." (A cleek is a hickory-shafted club with a long narrow head. It was used as a modern 2 iron and could also be used for putting.)

They began on some "extemporised links in Dean's Meadow" (now the cricket club) according to the writer of Dr. Standring's obituary. But a more satisfactory location was needed. Guy Pemberton tells us that he played "in 1894 when he [Dr. Standring] laid out the first nine hole course in the three fields between Bury End and the Kennels. The greens were about 10 feet square, roughly mown and rolled but not levelled". The photographs show this was indeed an accurate description and the barn which is in the background can still be identified at Bury End.

This ground was not ideal for a golf course – it is heavy and wet as well as being quite level. Mr. Les Arnold, our veteran member to whom this history is indebted for many recollections, thinks that the farmer wanted to plant cereal on the land so the golfers had to find "fresh woods and pastures new". No record exists of which way round this earliest course was played, Bury End to the Kennels or vice versa. Les favours the Kennels as the starting point, which does seem likely, because of its greater accessibility in the middle of the village.

Bury End c.1896

Dr. Standring on the tee, Bury End

Dr. Standring holds the flag, Bury End

After two years the course was moved to three fields on the hillside below the Tower, near Clump Farm. "A very sporting course", says Mr. Pemberton. It was this tower, a local folly, which became the emblem of Broadway Golf Club.

During this period one or two matches were being played. The very first mention of Broadway Golf Club was a report in the *Evesham Journal*, for Saturday, December 15th, 1894.

Golf Broadway v. Alcester, 8th December, Mr. A. E. Williams team. Played on the new links at Broadway on Saturday, 8th December and won by Broadway by 12 holes.

Dr. C. T. Standring	0	Mr. A. E. Williams	0
Mr. J. F. Campbell	0	Mr. E. A. Jephcott	0
Mr. C. T. Smith	12	Mr. H. G. Eastwood	0
Mr. B. Baldwin	0	Mr. E. Jones	4
Mrs. Standring	3	Mr. H. Overbury	0
Mr. R. Colomb	1	Mr. L. James	0
	16		4

An old method of scoring was used; the game was not over until the full 18 holes had been played and the result was the difference in the number of holes won. It was therefore theoretically possible for a player to win or lose 18 to 0.

Dr. Standring must have been convinced that his venture was a success because with membership standing at 36, he applied to have the club instituted on April 18th, 1895 with himself as captain and a Mr. C. T. Smith as honorary secretary.*

EQUIPMENT

Mr. Pemberton remarks, "It was, of course, the days of gutty balls, and those we got were mostly of the inferior kind. The very best was the Silvertown, price 1 shilling; we used to play mostly with a 4d ball with a red ring round it, which very often split when you struck it and there was a rule in force in those days, that if the ball split up, you played the largest portion from where it lay. I have often had to chivy a large piece of ball with a flat side into the hole. We bought a mould and melted down faulty balls and recast them".

RULES

The rules of the Royal and Ancient were universally accepted at about the time Broadway was founded. No ordinary club golfer in the world knows and understands every clause, sub clause, appendix and nuance of the

* This information was provided by Peter Lewis, British Golf Museum, St. Andrews, from the Golf Annual, 1897.

modern rules of golf. However in these early days they were simpler. As nowadays, clubs had their own local rules and we can see a list of Broadway's on the front of the earliest fixture card to be found.

It is interesting to note number 5: "Bye laws posted in the club house", which means they must have had a building in the days they played below the Tower but we know nothing else of it. Also notice "Play six days a week" – Sunday play was not acceptable. This rule was still in force in 1901. In a letter sent out by Dr. Standring (now honorary secretary) we read of a proposed new course "The links will be open for play throughout the year (Sundays excepted)". At this time, of course, inland golf was considered to be a winter game, summer being taken up by tennis and cricket because of the difficulties of upkeep of a course during the growing months.

FIRST PERIOD 1894–1901

1860, arrival of railway in Evesham leading to
    change in social structure of Broadway.
1894, Dr. C. T. Standring comes to village.
1894, first golf match against Alcester.
1895, official founding of Club Bury End to Kennels.
1897, move up hillside from Kennels to the Tower.

RULES.

1—Royal and Ancient Club of St. Andrews.

2—Play six days a week.

3—Subscriptions—
  Gentlemen £1 1s.
  Ladies 10s.6d.
  Visitors 2s.6d. per week.
  Visitors 5s. per month.

4—Candidates for election must be proposed and seconded by 3 members.

5.—Bye-laws posted in Club House.

MATCHES.

1900.

Jan. 10	Cotswold Golf Club	Stow.
.. 20	Alcester	Alcester.
Feb. 3	Stratford	Stratford.
.. 17	Evesham	Evesham.
Mar. 3	Stratford	Broadway.
.. 17	Evesham	Broadway.
Apr. 7	Alcester	Broadway.
.. 18	Cotswold Golf Club	Br'dway.

BROADWAY GOLF CLUB, 1899-1900.

President :
I. AVERILL, ESQ.

Vice-Presidents :
LORD ELCHO.
VISCOUNT LIFFORD.
RT HON. A. J. BALFOUR, M.P.
EDGAR FLOWER ESQ.
W. S. BARRETT ESQ.
F. H. JACKSON ESQ.
A. F. de NAVARRO, ESQ.

Hon. Sec. & Treas. :
C. T. STANDRING, ESQ.
THE LAURELS, BROADWAY.

Chapter Two

Vaulting Ambition 1901–11

IMMEDIATE PROBLEMS

EVEN though membership had dropped from 36 to 27 by the turn of the century, the doctor and his friends felt the time was right for a move. They had an ambitious scheme for an 18-hole course on the north side of the main road. So with a balance in the bank of 8/9d they embarked on growth.

BROADWAY GOLF CLUB 1900 – 1901						
	£.	s.	d.		£.	s.	d.
Viscount Lifford	1	1	0	Rent	7	0	0
Major Drummond	1	1	0	Returfing	3	6	9
Captain Rodgers	1	1	0	Wages	9	0	0
W.S. Barrett	1	1	0	Telegrams	1	10	0
A. Renfrew	1	1	0	(matches etc)			
E. Flower	1	1	0	Rubber stamp		2	6
S. Flower	1	1	0	Typewriting		7	6
F.H. Jackson	1	1	0	Flags		1	0
A.F. de Navarro	1	1	0	Club cards		6	6
C.T. Standring	1	1	0	Bogey cards		10	0
Colonel Halkett		10	6	Mending roller		3	0
Revd C.A. Baker		10	6	Postage &			
Revd C.O. Bartlett		10	6	small expenses		5	0
E.P. Prince		10	6				
P. Prince		10	6		22	12	9
R.M. Castle		10	6				
T.E. Pemberton		10	6				
G. Pemberton		10	6				
Mrs Rodgers		10	6				
Mrs Barrett		10	6				
Mrs Standring		10	6				
Miss Morgan		10	6				
Miss P. Morgan		10	6				
S. Rodgers		5	0				
R. Pierse Duncombe		5	0				
T. Pearson		2	6				
E. Hewitt		2	6				
	18	1	6				
Balance 1899	5	0	0				
	23	1	6				
	22	12	9				
		8	9				

The Links will be open for play on Saturday, September 28th.

The annual General Meeting will be held at "the Laurels" on Wednesday, October 2nd at 5p.m.

Business:- To elect officers for the coming season.
To pass the accounts.
To consider the report of Hobley (Cheltenham Professional) respecting the construction of new links on the north side of the main road.

C.T. Standring (Hon:Sec:)

The very first extant minute book gives a report of the 6th AGM held at the Laurels on October 3rd 1901. Only four out of 27 members were present with Lord Lifford in the chair. The name Renfrew first crops up here. Mr. Renfrew was a keen golfer and the local vet. The Renfrew family kept a continuity of membership until very recent times. It was decided unanimously to try to secure new links on the north side of the London Road, "commencing in the field opposite Mr. de Navarro's house". This is Court Farm, situated at the very end of the village. The main object of this meeting was to consider the report of Hobley, the Cheltenham professional, regarding the construction of the new course. The land they wanted to lease was owned by Mr. Chadwick of Farncombe House (now the headquarters of Group 4). "Starting in the top field on the left hand side of the village going up, it stretched away up to the top of Willersey Hill and back again", says Guy Pemberton.

They hoped to keep the course open for play throughout the year – an unrealistic hope as it was to turn out.

The first problem to be overcome was how to raise the money and it was decided to send out a letter asking for donations with the hope of obtaining new members. The honorary secretary sent out 50.

The minutes tell us that it was Henry Wilson, the professional at Rhos-on-Sea, not Hobley of Cheltenham, who was employed to supervise the construction of the course. According to the *Victoria History of Worcestershire* the course had a bogey of 80.

At a special meeting on November 11th, 1901, Dr. Standring announced that he had received only two replies, which caused "considerable discussion regarding the best method of raising the sum required for the construction of the links".

Broadway Golf Club.

THE LAURELS,
BROADWAY,
November 1st, 1901.

Dear Sir,

    I am requested by the Committee to inform you that they have been able to secure the New Links (beginning at the field opposite MR. DE NAVARRO's house) as proposed at the Annual General Meeting in September.

    It is estimated that the cost of construction will be about £100 and the annual expenditure about £50.

    Will you kindly let me know if you will contribute to the Ground Fund and what amount, and if you can give me the names of any likely members for election.

    The Subscription for 1902 has been provisionally fixed at £2 2 0.

    The Links will be 18 holes and will be open for play throughout the year (Sundays excepted).

    Members will have the privilege of introducing visitors at 5/- a week.

    MR. DE NAVARRO has kindly undertaken the entire expense of employing the professional HENRY WILSON to supervise the construction of the links.

    MR. WILSON declares that the links are as attractive as any inland course he knows in England or Scotland and can be made as good.

Faithfully yours,
CHARLES STANDRING,
Hon. Sec.

P.S. I have already received one donation of £10.

Sixteen new members eventually submitted their names and were unanimously elected, including the author J. M. Barrie, of Peter Pan fame, as well as Arthur Balfour, who had been a vice president for some time but, one can assume, was not a paid-up member.

The subscription was set at:

New members   £2. 2s. 0d.
Ladies   £1. 1s. 0d.
Original members   £1. 1s. 0d.

The balance sheet of September 1902 shows money was raised with a small surplus of £15. 16s. 1d.

Receipts.

Donations.

	£	s	d
Lord Elcho	25	10	0
J. Carlisle	25	0	0
A. F. de Navarro	10	0	0
Capt. Rodgers	5	5	0
Lord Lifford	5	0	0
W. S. Barrett	5	0	0
S Flower	5	0	0
Courtland Palmer	5	0	0
Lord Redesdale	5	0	0
Edgar Flower	3	3	0
A. Renfrew	3	3	0
Lady Hilda McNeill	2	2	0
R. S. P. Duncombe	2	2	0
Rev. F. A. Morgan	1	1	0
Capt. Treherne	1	1	0
Alfred Parsons	1	1	0
Chas. Duncombe	1	1	0
J. Prichard	1	1	0
	£106	10	0

Subscriptions.

	£	s	d
Lord Elcho	2	2	0
Ego Charteris	2	2	0
A. F. de Navarro	2	2	0
H. P. Greene	2	2	0
Capt. Rodgers	2	2	0
Dr. Standring	2	2	0
F. Kenyon Stow	2	2	0
J. Carlisle	2	2	0
Alf. Parsons	2	2	0
R. S. P. Duncombe	2	2	0
W. S. Barrett	2	2	0
R. Cordell	2	2	0
Lord Lifford	2	2	0
S. Flower	2	2	0
A. Renfrew	2	2	0
H. Patten	2	2	0
A. H. Sharp	2	2	0
Rev. Collins Ashwin	2	2	0
J. Wormald	2	2	0

	£	s	d
Rt. Hon. A. J. Balfour	2	2	0
J. Cordell	2	2	0
W. Neilson	1	1	0
E. Pemberton	1	1	0
F. H. Jackson	1	1	0
Guy Pemberton	1	1	0
Col. Halkett	1	1	0
Rev. C. A. Baker	1	1	0
J. R. H. Burland	1	1	0
J. M. Barrie	1	1	0
J. Bowers	1	1	0
E. Walsh	1	1	0
	£54	12	0

Subscriptions.—Ladies.

	£	s	d
Lady Hilda McNeill	1	1	0
Mrs. de Navarro	1	1	0
Mrs. Barrett	1	1	0
Mrs. Rodgers	1	1	0
Mrs. Duncombe	1	1	0
Mrs. Standring	1	1	0
Miss Morgan	1	1	0
	£7	7	0

Visitors.

	£	s	d
H. Herkomer	0	10	0
P. E. O. Marriott	0	8	0
A. Prichard	0	5	0
F. Stevenson	0	5	0
Miss Bruce	0	2	0
Miss Heneage	0	4	0
	£1	14	0

	£	s	d
Donations	106	10	0
Subscriptions	54	12	0
" Ladies	7	7	0
Visitors	1	14	0
	£170	3	0

Expenditure.

	£	s	d
Labour Wages—Levelling, Turfing, Mowing, &c.	132	8	8
Rent, Old Links	2	0	0
Clubroom at Farm	0	10	0
Railway Sleepers	3	18	0
Manure	1	12	6
Wire and Tightener	8	7	2
Paint	1	16	6
Sundries	1	19	0
18 Holes and Cutter	2	17	6
Mower	1	3	6
Ironwork Rollers	1	13	6
Repairs	1	11	6
Mats, Turf Cutter, Stile, &c.	0	19	10
Sand	0	7	0
Rent, Mr. Chadwick	10	10	0
Rent, Mr. Gillson	2	0	0
Agreement, Mr. New	2	3	0
Tools, "Badger"	0	17	0
Iron, &c., "Roberts"	1	3	6
Stone Rollers "Gill"	1	12	3
Hut, Stakes, &c., "Vizzard"	5	2	8
Printing	1	6	0
	185	19	1
	170	3	0
Balance due to Treasurer September 29, 1902	£15	16	1

THE NEW COURSE

However, the preparation and opening of an 18-hole course did not bring the hoped-for golf Utopia.

A difficulty faced by all early clubs was the rapid growth of grass and weeds, especially thistles during spring and summer months. Furthermore the type of ground they were on was particularly prone to infestation by rabbits which, as we still know, are particularly fond of digging holes in turf!

In 1902 it was decided to form a green committee and revise the bogey score and handicaps. In fact there were constant revisions of the bogey score, no doubt due to changes of the course route and other factors.

In an effort to keep the rabbits at bay, a tar line was set round each green, but we can assume that damage had already been done because holes 16 and 5 had to be returfed. At the same time sand and soot was sprinkled on some of the greens. (I have mentioned this to our present course manager. He says that he can understand the sand but not the soot.) Rails had to be put around the last green, probably to keep sheep at bay. This led to an addition to the rules in 1904 "that a ball striking the prop or rails surrounding the last green could be replaced without penalty".

The green was altered according to conditions (in these early days the term green meant the whole of the course, not just the putting areas). On November 11th, 1905 we read of "1st to rough field between 17 and 18 making no 2 no 1 and no 17 no 16 and shorten the grass mown to 18 by 20 yards". The following year was even more complicated: "The Hon. Sec. proposed no 4 as no 1 and play through to 13 as 5 and finish on a new green in Lower Bibsey". The final arrangement was:

```
Play    4  as   1
        5  as   2
        6  as   3
        7  as   4
Making a new green for no 5
       14 as   6
       15 as   7
       16 as   8
       17 as   9
Making a new green nearer to the club.
```

And if you think this sounds difficult and bewildering, I entirely agree! These early members were continually troubled by the long grass. What was the most cost effective and efficient way of dealing with it? The dilemma was between "summer keep" (which is allowing animals to graze it) or mowing for hay. Sheep would obviously bring other problems with them. Opinion seesawed over what to do. In 1903 the committee decided not to bid for grass keep but to arrange a price with the tenants for all that could be mown during the summer months. A dray for mowing was purchased and in April, 1904, a pony for pulling the mower. These problems were to bedevil the club for many years. It was beyond their resources not only to keep 18 holes open for the year, but hardly ever at all.

An interesting piece was found in the *Birmingham Post*, 1906, regarding a query on rules.

The Broadway Club

A query recently submitted to the Rules of Golf Committee by the Broadway (Worcestershire) Club serves as a striking indication of the difference of the conditions under which the game has to be played upon inland courses as compared with those which prevail over those happier seaside links for which the rules were originally formulated. What does St. Andrews know about mud, in which we in this part of the world are more or less up to our eyes during the winter months? It was mud which brought about the discussion at Broadway. The query sent to St. Andrews was as follows... "A and B are playing C and D. At the 6th tee B drives, slips, and misses the ball, leaving it on the tee. A fetches the coconut mat 3 yards away, and drives the ball on to the green. Is A justified in fetching the mat for a firm stand on the tee? Are A and B disqualified? Do A and B lose the hole for moving something more than a club's length away?" The reply received was: "My committee have decided that A is not within his rights in getting the mat. The ball is in play. A and B lose the hole". The same decision had also been given by Dr. Charles Standring, Broadway's energetic honorary secretary, before submitting the query to the ruling powers.

The £200 Golf Tournament. Left to right: Braid, Taylor, Mayo and Duncan, who competed for the prize

CHARLES MAYO

At this point it seems relevant to mention the first professional, not only because he was the first but also because Broadway Golf Club is distinguished in that in 1903 they gave notice to leave to a man who became one of the leading golfers of his day. In May 1903 "Dr. Standring reported satisfactory arrangements with Mayo the pro, 17/6d a week salary, 1/- for 9 holes coaching and 2/6d a dozen for golf balls". However by September 1903, the secretary was reporting on "the unsatisfactory condition of the links". "It was unanimously decided to give Mayo a fortnight's notice to leave and engage a groundsman at 16/- per week". Charles Mayo became a leading professional just prior to World War I, nearly in the class of Vardon, Braid, Taylor and Duncan.

He was considered an outstanding foursomes player, especially when teamed with George Duncan. He was also considered one of the slowest players of the time whilst Duncan was felt to be the fastest player, so no doubt there was some interesting golf to watch. In fact they played against each other at Broadway on May 2nd, 1914.

After leaving Broadway Mayo went on to Bridgenorth and then Burhill, Surrey, before emigrating to the USA in 1919. He returned to Broadway in 1908 to marry Rose Jones, the daughter of "Pecker" Jones, the Broadway carpenter who was to build the 1911 clubhouse.

In the late nineteenth century conditions were difficult for professionals. Many worked for poor clubs which could not afford to pay a reasonable retaining fee and others were attached to powerful clubs which could demand almost impossible hours and conditions of work. This was the situation which led to the founding of the PGA in 1901. Poor conditions of work encouraged any pro with ability to emigrate to the USA, like Charles Mayo. However, when he returned for visits, he would turn out in the club team. *Birmingham Post*, October, 1919:

On Wednesday a team from Kidderminster played a Broadway team, each side winning 4 matches. C. H. Mayo the professional, home from the States, played for Broadway against J. Fox, the Kidderminster professional. The game which was watched by many interested spectators, was won by C. H. Mayo by 6 and 4. Afterwards a foursome was played by J. N. Fox and A. Austin (Kidderminster) and C. H. Mayo and Dr. Alexander (Broadway), the latter winning by 2 holes, Mayo finishing with 2 and 3 at the 17th and 18th holes.

CONTINUED UPKEEP OF COURSE

In September 1903, with a new groundsman, it was decided to keep ten holes open for October and November, and postpone work until November on the top nine. They hoped at this time to play eighteen holes January, February, March and April in which it seems they may have succeeded, although bad weather in February postponed the Evesham match and the February bogey until March. April 1904 no doubt found the grass shooting up once more and "it was proposed that the summer course should start at 17 and finish at 18 leaving out 1, 2, 3, 4, 10, 11, 12". Without a plan of the course it is difficult to imagine how this was done but it must have detracted from the golf.

On April 14th, 1905, it was decided that again the course must be closed from May 1st to November 1st. The groundsman was given notice to leave for this period but the fences should be strengthened with extra posts and wire and he be paid 7/- a week through the summer to supervise the work. By 1908, at the AGM, regret was being expressed that the links were not better kept in the summer. "Several visitors complained". Visitors were an important part of income since Broadway had become more accessible with the arrival of the railway in 1904 and in 1905 it was reported that visitors contributed more than £20 in fees. The complaints were due to the same old problem – long grass which they could not afford to cut "as the cost was 18/- an acre". Clearly the 18 holes ambition on difficult terrain with limited mechanical aids available was too onerous a task even for the redoubtable Dr. Standring and his committee.

LANDLORDS, TENANTS, LEASES

The golf club, for many years to come, was dependent on the goodwill of the various owners and tenants of Farncombe House. Some of these imposed conditions on granting a lease, for example that their guests should be allowed to play free of charge. There were to be repercussions as late as the 1950s.

The first landlord of the 1901 course was a Mr. Chadwick. Agreements had to be reached not only with him but also with the various tenant farmers, and the Capital and Counties Bank in Broadway (now Goblets Wine Bar). In 1901 the bank agreed that work on the new course should start and the honorary secretary was authorised to offer 10/- per hole annual rent. Agreements took months to draw up and sign and the club never managed to obtain a long lease. Haggling with the tenants was common. In May 1903 a Mr. Dease is claiming 10/- per green but 2/6d per green was eventually agreed. At the same time the club agreed to pay 22/6d per acre for grass cut in Lower Bibsey (to put this in context our present 5th tee is Bibsey Spur). March 1904 saw Mr. Dease after more money. The club said they were unable to pay anything further for thistle mowing as they had already paid for grass mowing. A walk across this early course still shows the prevalence of thistles.

A name which appears several times in the minutes is Mr. Wells. In September 1903 he was unanimously elected an honorary member; in April 1904 it was decided to interview Mr. Wells regarding "the continuance of summer play". Mr. Wells replied that he wanted to be a *subscribing* member. He suggested putting iron supports round the 18th green and furthermore offered to erect a rustic club room instead of the present hut. "The Secretary gladly accepted the offer and asked Mr. Wells's acceptance of the hut in exchange". When everyone else was paying £2. 2s. 0d. subscription, Mr. Wells paid £10. 0s. 0d. On July 4th, 1906, Mr. Wells asked for greens to

17

be removed from Top Farm. He promised to compensate and move the clubhouse, make four new greens and contribute £10 a year for three years. It was puzzling why this man should have had such a say in the club. The answer was revealed in Dr. C. C. Houghton's history of Broadway, "A poor boy living at Alveston, near Stratford-upon-Avon, at the end of the last century set out for the United States to make his fortune. He did – he invented Quaker Oats – and came back to his native land; he bought Top Farm. His name was Wells". He became a philanthropist – no doubt the golf club committee felt it well worth their while to carry out his wishes, but it must have been a nuisance to have to change a green and the position of the clubhouse for reasons other than improving golfing facilities. Eventually the tenancy of Farncombe passed into the hands of the Skidmore Barretts who played an active part in the affairs of the golf club.

GOLF

Throughout all the vicissitudes the club continued to play regular matches.

Evesham Journal, February 28th, 1904

Golf
Chastleton Hill v. Broadway
Played at Chastleton

Broadway		Chastleton Hill	
Dr. Standring	8	Capt. C. G. Becher	0
A. Renfrew	6	Capt. W. Wyld	0
Rev. C. A. Baker	4	C. Richardson	0
H. Patten	1	J. S. Chappell	0
	19		0

Similarly matches are reported against Moreton, Evesham and Stratford with varying success.

The club also played a regular monthly bogey competition, the winner of which received a trophy. A bogey was the score a good player, but not a long hitter, should score – quite different from the modern meaning of bogey from the USA – one over.

It is said that the march "Colonel Bogey" was so named because it was written during a round of golf!

Birmingham Post, January 21st 1905 –

Broadway Golf Club

On Friday Mr. Neilson played off the tie for the November Cup against Dr. Standring, they having tied twice previously, and succeeded in coming in 5 up to Colonel Bogey".

Each member was entitled to take out a card to be played on a designated day of the month and these matches were regularly reported in the local press.

Broadway Golf Club

The monthly November bogey competition was played on Saturday, in wet weather. Ten members took out cards with the following result.

	H'cap
H. G. Clegg	16 + 4
Spencer Flower	14 – 1
Clive Smith	10 – 2
C. T. Standring	10 – 2
A. Johnsson	10 – 5
Guy Pemberton	18 – 6

The rest were no returns.

A stroke of luck located the present whereabouts of the bogey prize for this competition. It is in the possession of Mrs. R. E. Stokes of Broadway and is a pewter tankard inscribed "Broadway Golf Club, November, 1903". From the above cutting, she could be told it was won by H. G. Clegg. The Clegg family were influential members of Broadway Golf Club for some years.

In 1906 it was decided to try two bogey returns in each month for the six winter months, and award prizes at the end of April but only the £2. 2s. 0d. members should be eligible for bogey prizes. On February 6th, 1905, the *Birmingham Gazette* reported the new course record set by Dr. Standring – a round of 76 in a three ball match.

New Record for Broadway

Dr. Standring has been distinguishing himself at Broadway, a pretty Worcestershire course, situated 300 to 750ft above sea level. Playing in a three-ball match the other day, he holed the round in 76 – three strokes better than the previous record. His figures are worth setting out in detail. They are: 4, 4, 3, 4, 6, 4, 5, 4, 3, 6, 5, 4, 3, 5, 4, 4, 3, 5. We can recall in the early days of the course, how Lord Elcho's round of 80 was considered a remarkable performance, and when B. Sayers jun., accomplished 78, it was thought the summit of golfing skill had been reached. By and by one stroke was knocked off Lord Elcho's amateur record, and 79 held the field till Saturday, when Dr. Standring made it look quite a big figure.

In 1910 the 5/- fee for the bogey competitions was for two rounds for men, ladies 1/- for one round – rather a high figure when compared with the £2. 2s. 0d. subscription. Handicaps were revised to bring them in line with surrounding clubs.

In these early days both ladies and men were eligible to play in competitions and matches, although there is no evidence of ladies' scores except in the first-ever reported match in 1894 when Mrs. Standring was in the team. When one considers that both the 1897–1901 and the 1901–11 courses were laid out on what can only be described as mountain goat country, when golf was played mostly in winter with the vagaries of wind and rain we get in the hills, one wonders how ladies managed to play at all in the cumbersome style of dress they were obliged to wear. Skirts were bound with leather to make it easier to clean off the mud and sleeves were so wide one wonders how they managed to see the ball and, of course, a hat was required dress. Even so the balance sheets show a fairly steady number of lady members.

FINANCE AND MEMBERSHIP

We do not know the exact costs of the earlier courses but after 1901 the minutes tell of the constant need of money for wages, upkeep of the course and rent to both the owner of the land and the tenant farmers, as well as fees to lawyers for the drawing up of agreements.

Annual expenditure was expected to double to about £50. 0s. 0d. on the opening of the new links in 1901. The appeal in the honorary secretary's letter did not produce an immediate response although by 1902 £106. 10s. 0d. had been raised which, along with doubled subscriptions, raised £170. 3s. 0d., which did not quite cover costs. A minute on September 29th, 1902 showed the club to be "in the red" by £15. 16s. 1d.

			Income	Expenses		Balance
1901	18 men	5 ladies	£23. 1.6	£22.12. 9	+	8. 9
1902	31	7	£170. 3.0	£185.19. 1	–	£15.16. 1
1903	34	11	£83. 9.6	£107.17.10	–	£24. 8. 4
1904	38	10	£104.17.6	£112. 9. 5	–	£7.11.11
1905	27	9	£80.15.6	£74.16. 6	+	£5.19. 0
1906	23	7	£76. 3.0	£75.15. 4	+	7. 8
1907	16	7	£74.18.0	£74.18. 0	=	
1908	33	9	£82.10.0	£67. 2. 3	+	£15. 7. 9
1909	28	8	£94.17.3	£71.16. 2	+	£23. 1. 1
1910	28	5	£79 .9.7	£72. 4. 6	+	£7. 5. 1
1911	37	6	£156.18.1	£172.11. 7	–	£15.13. 6

In fact the club never seemed very well off, just managing to scrape by most of the time. At certain periods they worried about this but in spite of the wealth of most members, they did not charge high subscriptions as a solution to their problems. The subscription remained static at £2. 2s. 0d. for men and £1. 1s. 0d. for ladies for many years. They preferred to raise money by donation or by functions such as the Gymkhana organised by Lady Hilda McNeil.

Standard, July 30th, 1904 Gymkhana

Three years ago it was found practicable to remove the golf links, which had existed for five years below Broadway tower. A suitable site was secured on the Farncombe estate and the Top Farm. Under the superintendence of Wilson, the professional from Colwyn Bay, the eighteen hole course was laid out. The membership at once increased to about fifty, and at the end of twelve months the committee of the club found there was a deficit of £25 on the cost of outlay. Since then the club has continued to exist, but the number of members has not increased. At the committee meeting held last March the committee had seriously to consider the closing of the links, as, in addition to the expenses, groundsman, rent, etc., there was the amount to be paid for mowing the grass between the greens. Happily this was averted and Lady Hilda McNeil came to the assistance of the committee by offering to organise a gymkhana, sports, etc. This suggestion the committee gladly accepted. Friday was the day fixed, this being the only day upon which the co-operation of the polo players of the Stratford Club could be secured. The event proved a remarkable success, and the proceeds amounted to nearly £50. The details of the events are appended below. The committee have to acknowledge the gift of a club pavilion which has been presented by Mr. T. E. Wells, and it only remains for a greater number of visitors to join the club to secure its prosperity in the future.

Some of the events are then described for example "Menagerie race: Goose driven by Mr. Duncombe 1: cockerel, driven by Mr. Miller 2". Alongside came the more conventional tug of war and egg and spoon on ponies.

A most amusing item of the programme was a mounted hockey match between two teams mounted on hobby horses which were constructed at the Broadway Stud Farm and trained by Mr. Pierse Duncombe. This evoked roars of laughter, and the novelty was much appreciated. The Broadway Band played a selection of music during the afternoon, and dancing was kept up with vigour till 10pm. The prizes which were varied, useful, and valuable, were presented by Mrs. de Navarro, Lady Hilda McNeil, Mrs. Barrett, Mrs. Pemberton, and others. They were gracefully distributed by Lady Hilda McNeil. The Earl of Gainsborough proposed a hearty vote of thanks to her, and this was seconded by Mr. de Navarro and carried with cheers. The catering was in the hands of Mr. Russell, of the Lygon Arms Hotel, who was himself unfortunately ill in bed.

So it would seem that these people knew how to enjoy themselves without too many inhibitions.

Another source of income were the concerts organised by the de Navarros, hardly a satisfactory way of financing a golf club.

It is not surprising that by 1908 the committee was seeking to put the club on a more stable footing and a move to the top of the hill was suggested, where the terrain was flatter and there were no tenant farmers to harass the golf. Up to this point I think it is reasonable to say that in spite of effort and many "good

21

ideas", the club was making no real progress. The minutes are scant and tantalising in what they do *not* tell us. There is no report of the discussion which must have taken place before the decision came to move yet again. Whose idea was it? However, if the idea had not been implemented, it is possible that the club would not have survived its hundred years.

Perhaps it came as a shock to the committee to receive a letter from Charles Mayo saying he was "prepared to extend and supervise improvement of the links and was prepared to put £500 down if an extra 40 members could be secured". As can be imagined "considerable discussion ensued" and a sub committee was set up to investigate. However by March 12th, 1910, Charles had changed his mind and the matter was dropped. But only temporarily as once more the advice of Mr. Hobley of Cheltenham was sought. He had no hesitation in recommending the club to extend the course to the top fields. He said he could lay out a very good nine hole course using two existing holes, which would be playable all year round and not require very much mowing outside the greens. He could confidently say that the course would be playable by April, 1911. Thus we have the beginning of modern times – the first nine holes as we know them now. The two existing holes mentioned were our present sixth and seventh.

SECOND PERIOD 1901–11

1901, move to new course laid out by Henry Wilson.
1902, formed first greens committee.
1903, Charles Mayo employed as professional.
1904, purchase of pony for pulling mower.
1905, first Sunday play.
1908, thoughts of moving again.
1910, offer from Mayo to help.
1910, advice of Hobley, Cheltenham professional for new links.

Chapter Three

On Top of the Hill 1911–24

YET ANOTHER NEW COURSE

ALTHOUGH the minutes continue to lack detail, it is quite obvious that plans went ahead immediately. The occupiers of Farncombe House were the Skidmore Barretts but the estates, including Willersey Hill Farm were still owned by Mr. Chadwick with whom a new lease had to be negotiated. The club was able to take over 75 acres on the top of the hill (unfortunately still on a short lease) on land which was dry. A glance at the Ordnance Survey map shows the number of springs on the side of the hill compared with the top.

Being over 800ft above sea level the grass did not grow so profusely (hence Mr. Hobley's promise of being able to lay out a course which would not need much mowing outside the greens). Another advantage was there was only one tenant farmer to deal with, a Mr. Cotterill, himself on an annual tenancy. There are no details given but there must have been hope that their own lease could be extended, which would have been an incentive for development. In January 1911, it was planned to take the club hut to pieces and move it to the 1st tee. With the enthusiasm which these early members constantly maintained "it was decided to hold an open competition directly the frost gave". The *Birmingham Post*, March 17th, 1911 ran an article on the club and the alterations and improvements.

Golf Notes – The Course at Broadway

The alterations and improvements to the Broadway links, upon which the committee have been engaged for some time, with the assistance and advice of Hobley, professional to the Cheltenham club, have now been completed, and all concerned are to be congratulated upon the excellent results of their labours. The course is one of nine holes, the first one being 325 yards long, with a very good green. The second is 290 yards, and here a large new putting green has been made. The third is an iron-shot hole, 120 yards, uphill and over gorse and a stone wall. The next is the longest hole of the round, 433 yards, with the drive guarded by a bunker on either side, and similar pitfalls to the right and left of the green. There is again, no lack of difficulties at the fifth, 307 yards, or at the sixth, 265 yards, where to reach the green – a large and good one – an old, disused quarry has to be carried. On the way to the seventh, 321 yards, a stone wall has to be negotiated, and the green is well guarded. At the eighth, 238 yards, another wall makes the approach shot difficult; while the last hole, 125 yards finishes near the Club Hut ... Unlike the earliest course laid out at Broadway, upon which the activity of the mountain goat was necessary for its complete enjoyment, the present green is not fatiguing, and there is not a wet patch in the whole round ... The club though a small one, can put a good match team into the field. On Saturday they went to Moreton-in-Marsh, and beat the local players by 7 to 2½. It is a pity that among the club's bye laws there is one allowing a ball to be lifted and cleaned on the putting green, more particularly as the course is a dry one. This practice, which obtains here and there, usually on greens with a clay subsoil, is one to be strongly discouraged, as it is opposed to the fundamental principle of the game, which is the ball must not be handled between tee and hole, except on those rare occasions provided for by the Rules of Golf. Mud on the ball is one of those drawbacks to the game which inland golfers have to put up with as philosophically as they can, and it is better to regard it as a rub of the green than to adopt a practice which is contrary to the best traditions of golf.

It would be easy to assume that the club hut was moved to somewhere in the region of its present position and this misunderstanding has prevailed in the past. However careful reading of the description in the newspaper shows this was not the case, the main clue being "The third is an iron shot hole 120 yards, uphill and over gorse and a stone wall". This hole no longer exists on the modern course but the tee was by the present 7th green and the green approximately in the region of the ladies' present 4th tee. The walk up was still visible and negotiable 35 years ago, along the side of the 7th. Time and growth of scrub have obliterated evidence although some old pen sketches show the steps. Thus the first hole mentioned was the modern 6th, the second the modern 7th (these were the two holes incorporated by Mr. Hobley from the 1901 course).

The club hut therefore, must have been re-erected somewhere behind our present 5th green or 6th tee. It can clearly be seen in the sketches reproduced on pages 49-53. To reach this starting point players had to negotiate the side of the hill from opposite Court Farm, just as they had been doing for the past nine years. Such a climb followed by 18 holes of golf must have been quite a feat. Nevertheless the course was played in this way until the beginning of 1912.

A NEW PAVILION

On January 24th, 1912 "the question of a pavilion at the Willersey Hill end of the Links" was considered by the committee. Again the minutes give no details of the discussion which must have taken place. Still being handwritten by the honorary secretary Dr. Standring, they are *very* difficult to read and certainly give the impression of being dashed off by a busy man. The wheel was to come full circle when a later honorary secretary, a man of many words, made rather extravagant use of the typewriter! It was certainly a common sense decision to build a new clubhouse near the road at the top of Willersey Hill. This resiting of the pavilion had another important effect because it meant that it was moved from Worcestershire into Gloucestershire and although the actual course incorporated parts of both counties, the position of the clubhouse determines to which county the club belongs from a golf point of view. Hence Broadway Golf Club qualified eventually to become a member of the Gloucestershire Golf Union.

The new position was of greater advantage for the owners of motor cars or horse transport which could be accommodated at Willersey Hill Farm (nowadays the Dormy House Hotel). When the railway touched Willersey visiting players were able to hire transport to the club. Arrangements were made with Bollands Garage, Willersey, to motor players up to the club at charges of 3s for two, 3s 6d for three and 4s for four players. Even so it remained fairly inaccessible.

Plans for the new pavilion were put in hand. Permission had to be sought from the landlord, Mr. Chadwick, and the details were left to a sub committee. Several estimates were obtained and it was eventually decided to give the work to H. Jones (the father-in-law of Charles Mayo). The pavilion was planned to be 20ft x 12ft with one door and two windows – cost £31-10s.

Opening of new pavilion 1912. Centre front: Dr. and Mrs. Strandring with daughter. Arthur Balfour in dark suit and cap next to Lady Elcho. Behind the rail "Pecker" Jones the carpenter, Harold Keyte the decorator

OPENING MATCH – CHANGE IN ORDER OF PLAY

The completion of the building was marked by a grand opening foursome match played by Mr. A. J. Balfour, Mr. Hugo Charteris, the eldest son of Lord Elcho, against Mr. Herbert Asquith, the second son of the prime minister (as well as being Lord Elcho's son-in-law) and Mr. Spenser Flower of the brewing family.

Originally, the club founder, Dr. Standring was to play but he had sprained his thumb and Mr. Flower substituted. The match was reported in both local and national press due to the presence of Mr. Balfour.

Daily Mail, March 25th 1912

Mr. Balfour's Foursome. Match at Broadway.
Mr. A. J. Balfour played in a foursome on the Broadway Golf Club's course, Worcestershire, but he and his partner, Mr. Hugo Charteris, the eldest son of Lord Elcho, were beaten by 3 up and 2 to play by Mr. Herbert Asquith, the second son of the Prime Minister and a son-in-law of Lord Elcho, and Mr. Spenser Flower.

The Broadway Golf Club is now playing on a nine-hole course laid out on a plateau on the top of the Cotswold Hills, and its only drawback is its inaccessibility. It is a long climb from anywhere and is not likely to become very popular with those who do not possess motorcars. The morning proved wet and blustery. Shortly after three o'clock in the afternoon Mr. Balfour arrived, accompanied by Lady Elcho, Mr. Charteris and Mr. H. Asquith.

Then follows detailed hole for hole description of the game.

A considerable crowd was rewarded by seeing an interesting match. The golf was always good. Mr. Charteris was the most brilliant of the four, but he was always striving to make up for what Mr. Balfour lost in length, and this told against his steadiness. Mr. Balfour was occasionally at fault but was generally very sound. Mr. Flower's local knowledge helped him. Mr. Asquith was very steady.

At the close of the game Mr. Balfour said he thought the course was a very attractive one and not so tiring as the Cleeve Hill course. He also considered the committee were wise in keeping to nine holes which could be kept in good order. Many present members will sympathise with Mr. Balfour, who said his game was somewhat hampered by the drizzling rain which affected his view through his glasses.

This foursomes match was played approximately in the way that the first nine are played today. A good description was found in the magazine *Midland Golfer* September, 1912.

Driest Course in England

Having been literally swamped out at our home club, and tired of plodding round the links wet through, we determined to accept the invitation of the hon. secretary of the Broadway Club to spend a weekend there. Well, certainly the links are rather ungetable but if you find the Fish Inn at the top of Broadway Hill and keep along the road to the left you come to Willersey Hill Farm. We left our little motor there, and found the clubhouse in the next field close to the road going to Saintbury Village.

A notice outside the club house says: "Visitors can obtain day tickets from the groundsman always on the links". Although it was raining pretty hard, we found the groundsman, who keeps the key of the house, and having paid for three days we started round. The 1st hole is about 360 yards crossing a stone wall, and the fairway is kept well mown: the green is very good: the 2nd hole is guarded well on the left by a disused quarry, the length is 265 yds. The 3rd hole is 320 and the 4th 475. Two bunkers have to be negotiated, a stone wall and a faggot hedge protected by wire. The 5th is a drop pitch hole only 125 yds, but it needs a very accurate shot to land on the green. The 6th is over a slight hill, and the green is well guarded by disused cart-ruts and gorse right and left: the 7th is 300 yds, and this green needs taking up and returfing: the 8th is 145 yds uphill over a stone wall, and the 9th is a long hole, 450 yds but needs more bunkers to make it interesting. So much for the course. We spent three very happy days here, and when the rain ceased obtained magnificent views over the West country to Malvern and Wales, and were sorry when our time was up to motor back to the smoky Black Country.

We feel that this new course only needs knowing to become more popular, and it is truly the driest course in England.

One or two of the walls have disappeared, for example the one across the 1st which is those days ran right across the 1st, 3rd and 4th fairways. The position is easily located, especially when the weather is dry. The 2nd tee was near today's 1st green and can still be found; the drive was down past the old disused quarry (today on the right of the 2nd, the repository of many a sliced ball, then on the left). The old 8th hole started life as the 3rd up over the gorse. The modern 8th was not built until much later.

Present-day golfers will certainly endorse the sentiment expressed by the *Evesham Journal* of the day about golf "on the top of the Cotswold Hills where the views are grand and the air strong and bracing".

On a summer's day there is surely nowhere more beautiful whilst the rigours of winter wind, rain and snow prove that Broadway is not for the faint-hearted golfer.

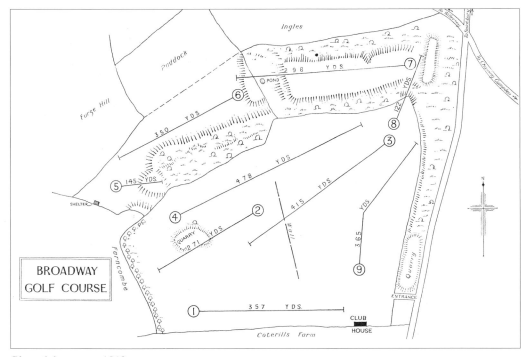

Plan of the course, 1912

UPKEEP OF COURSE

Whilst the move to the top made care of the course easier, general upkeep was still a priority. Mr. Hobley of Cheltenham was employed to keep an eye on the area and on November 9th, 1912, it was reported that he had been over "and recommended less rolling of the greens but daily sweeping, repairing all bad patches on the greens, returfing the 7th green, a faggot bunker between 2 and 4 and one to R & L of 3 and one R & L of 9".

Which raises the question, what is a faggot bunker? In the byelaws printed on the back of the balance sheets "hedge bunkers" are mentioned. "A ball lying in one of the artificial hedge bunkers must be lifted and dropped behind under a penalty of a stroke". Perhaps it is safe to assume that a "faggot bunker" and an "artificial hedge bunker" are one and the same. In those days the top of the hill was fairly bare and perhaps these bunkers were a quick and cheap way of creating a hazard to trap the bad shot.

A more professional approach was being taken to care for the course – tees and greens were constructed instead of a flat piece of a farmer's field being mowed for use. The 19th AGM reported that "All tees had received a good dressing of sea sand". A groundsman (NB not a professional) had necessarily been employed after Charles Mayo left, but by October 11th, 1913, the minutes report the serious illness of the groundsman H. Malin "who decided to give up the post". Help was sought from Mr. Hobley, who was unable to recommend a Cheltenham man. Out of 12 applications, Wm. Malin was appointed at 18s a week, no doubt a relation of H. Malin. However the choice was not a happy one because by December "The Secretary reported that the groundsman had been convicted for assault." The president severely reprimanded him and warned him that if anything occurred again he would get the sack! He must have taken the warning to heart and set about his job because by 1915 the greens "were better than ever". The committee decided to buy a light mowing machine in 1917 for the groundsman to mow the fairway. Looking at the first class condition of the fairways today, having just been cut by the latest, state of the art machine, it would be interesting if we could put these two machines side by side.

The club continued to let the grass keep to Mr. Cotterill, the tenant of

Club Handicap..........					Strokes against Bogey or in Match play..........					
Member's Name..........										
Hole	Length Yards	Bogey	Strokes Index	SCORE	Won + Lost - Halved O	Hole	Length Yards	Bogey	Strokes Index	SCORE	Won + Lost - Halved O
1	380	5	9			10	380	5	6		
2	271	4	13			11	271	4	14		
3	417	5	11			12	417	5	10		
4	510	5	3			13	510	5	2		
5	145	3	17			14	145	3	16		
6	350	5	5			15	350	4	4		
7	298	4	7			16	298	4	8		
8	122	3	15			17	122	3	18		
9	410	5	1			18	410	5	12		
T'ls	2903	38				T'ls	2903	38			

BOGEY RESULT :

Total length **5806** yards

MEDAL RESULT :

Holes Won ....   Out..........

Holes Lost ....   In ....

Resut _____   Total ....

Handicap ....

Marker's Signature..........   Net Score _____

Score card for 9 hole course

Willersey Hill farm, for £20 per annum "on condition that he undertook to keep up all walls, gates and fences etc."

But as had always been the case with the tenant farmers he was not too assiduous in fulfilling his part of the agreement and straying animals continued to be a problem. When the keep was next let to Mr. Jordan of Long Marston for the princely sum of £70 again his cattle and sheep caused damage to such an extent that the matter reached the hands of their respective solicitors! The club finally gave the management of the keep to Rightons estate agents of Evesham.

ADMINISTRATION OF THE CLUB

In these early years Broadway Golf Club was very much a self-help affair, advantageous regarding costs, but sometimes with problems from an efficiency standpoint. For example, whilst we are lucky to have minutes from 1901 when the 6th AGM was held, the numbering becomes confused when the minutes do not state which AGM was being held. Only the date is recorded, with the result that the sequential numbering is wrong. This error was compounded in the war years when occasionally there was no AGM and at other times two in one year. All this led to confusion over the true date of the founding of the club although Mr. Pemberton, in his memoirs, states he held a party to celebrate the first 50 years in 1944 but these memoirs were the private property of his widow, kindly lent for the purposes of this history. In actual fact the numbering is quite irrelevant; the proof of the founding date lay elsewhere.

The office of captain does not appear to have been as important then as now, not being mentioned in the minutes until October, 1922, when Dr. Standring was officially elected captain, after having given up the hon. sec. position. However, it seems he assumed the role from the beginning. The title president continued to be reserved for a man who would give prestige to the club. The real work fell on the shoulders of the treasurer and, more importantly, the hon. sec. This position was held by Dr. Standring for 26 years. Thus it was his influence which was dominant. During the war years, the club appeared to be struggling, perhaps because Dr. Standring had several official war time duties which took up his time and in about 1920 his wife became ill and died, a blow from which he never really recovered. Thus the way was open for someone else and the person who gradually came to the fore was Dr. Alexander. In his turn, he worked as hard and was as influential as his predecessor.

MORE PERSONALITIES

Perhaps the name best known to modern members is that of Mr. T. H. Lloyd, who was elected president from 1911 to 1921. He has remained a man of

some mystery but the fact that he was president shows the club considered him important, probably as a result of wealth and social influence. Mr. R. G. Stokes, a resident of Broadway, was able to tell us that he may have been a stockbroker. He lived at Pear Tree House, towards the top end of Broadway High Street, and also owned property in Scotland which he frequently visited for the shooting. It is just possible to visualise the man from these few facts. The minutes show that he attended meetings but give no evidence of any contribution he made except he donated what has come to be one of the club's major trophies, the Lloyd Cup.

On January 24th 1912, the secretary reported that he had received a handsome silver challenge cup from the president and proposed a hearty vote of thanks. It was carried unanimously, Mr. Patten saying the president had done a lot to stimulate interest in the club by the presentation. Mr. Lloyd in reply said he did not want any thanks but he hoped that by playing for the cup by match play each spring the members would find out who was the best. He agreed to pay £1 to the runner up each year for 5 years provided the committee secured 8 starters for the cup.

Thus his name found an important place in the archives. Mr. Lloyd disappeared quite suddenly from the scene; there is no vote of thanks recorded, no note of his resignation but after being re-elected President in October, 1919, the last mention of him dates from January 14th, 1920.

Mr. E. Kenyon Stow is noteworthy because, apart from being an active committee member for many years, he donated to the club "a Sheffield plate salver. It was decided to play for it medal play, quarterly." This salver is now the club championship plate. Mr. Stow also presented an ancient golf club for display. as can be seen in the cutting from the magazine *Midland Golfer* of December, 1914.

I wonder where it is now? The club does possess a few antique items, namely a Bussey bag made around 1900, a Hunter putter and a Dunn putter. Hunter was the professional at Royal Cinque Ports, 1890; Dunn was the professional at Royal Wimbledon Common, 1885; Geo Bussey & Co were manufacturers in London at the end of the last century.

Need for Capital

The various newspaper articles already quoted in this book all mention the inaccessibility of the club. The remoteness was a decided drawback. To increase capital, more members were needed but the surrounding area was

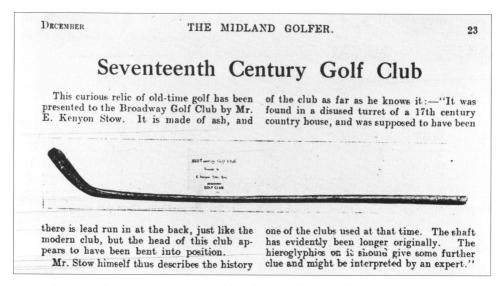

December THE MIDLAND GOLFER. 23

Seventeenth Century Golf Club

This curious relic of old-time golf has been presented to the Broadway Golf Club by Mr. E. Kenyon Stow. It is made of ash, and of the club as far as he knows it:—"It was found in a disused turret of a 17th century country house, and was supposed to have been

there is lead run in at the back, just like the modern club, but the head of this club appears to have been bent into position.

Mr. Stow himself thus describes the history one of the clubs used at that time. The shaft has evidently been longer originally. The hieroglyphics on it should give some further clue and might be interpreted by an expert."

sparsely populated compared with the position of the new clubs being founded nearer Birmingham – Olton and Kings Norton, for example. Their success was largely due to growth in industrial wealth. Dr. Standring started something of an advertising campaign.

Evesham Journal, December, 1910

The Secretary will be glad to receive the names of residents in Broadway, Campden and Blockley willing to join … green fees 1s a day, 5s a week, 17s 6d a month, £2 2s 0d a year.

It was decided to obtain books for day tickets for play for the groundsman and the Lygon and Noel Arms, Campden.

Green fees were certainly an important part of income. But although membership increased, the balance sheet of 1910–11 shows £15 13s 6d deficit – income £156 18s 1d against expenditure £172 11s 7d. Compare this with 1901–2 – income £170 3s 0d against expenditure £185 19s 1d – deficit £13 16s 1d. It could be deduced from this that no progress had been made but on the positive side they had a superior golf course, therefore better value for money.

Due to this need for funds, the golf club had to cease being a bastion of the upper classes and allow the local tradesman to be a member. May 20th, 1912:

The President stated he had received a letter signed by five residents in the village asking if they could play golf on certain days at a reduced subscription. It was eventually unanimously decided that a limited number of restricted members be elected to the privileges of the club each year with certain reservations.
1. They should have no voice in the management of the club.
2. They should not have the use of the clubhouse but should be allowed to use the lower hut.
3. That each name should be submitted to the committee for election.

4. That they should be allowed to play at any time except match days and competition days and Saturdays October–April that they should play on Saturday during May–September after 4 o'clock.
5. That they should not have the privilege of admitting friends.
6. That they should strictly observe the rules.
7. That the subscription be 10s 6d.

Thus was inaugurated what some clubs called the Artisan Section whereas at Broadway the term Village Players was used. The lower hut mentioned was the old pavilion which had been in use as the clubhouse when the course was on the side of the hill. It was not a hut specially built for themselves by these village players. It was eventually used as a weather shelter until about 1965. Les Arnold says this hut eventually caught fire and was destroyed but traces of it are still to be found, namely a few bits of iron among the trees beyond the fifth green. There are three trees in this patch of ground planted in memory of Jack Sutton, an old member, by Les Arnold and two friends to commemorate the many happy fourball games they had on Wednesday afternoons over a period of 20 years. Jack Sutton managed to achieve three hole-in-ones in these games.

Harold Keyte with Lloyd Cup and Standrinks Trophy, 1923

The most notable village player was Mr. Keyte, the local decorator, who was a first-class player and became a full member of the club. He won the Lloyd Cup two years running and eventually became captain of the club in 1930.

Another rule formulated in 1912 was that no member could introduce a visitor resident within four miles radius. Presumably it was thought that anyone so close should become a full member, with a positive effect on the bank balance.

As a publicity exercise an exhibition match was arranged in May, 1914 between George Duncan and Charles Mayo (who still had connections in the village). "It was decided not to charge gate money but to charge 2/6d for each vehicle."

This match was reported at length in the *Evesham Journal*, including the usual comments on the inaccessibility of the course and the magnificent views.

Golf – Duncan at Broadway.

The committee of the Broadway Golf Club provided a rare treat for golfing enthusiasts of the district on Saturday, when they arranged for a match between George Duncan of Hanger Hill, and C. H. Mayo of Burhill, to be played over their course last Saturday. It was a matter of surprise that more golfers did not take advantage of the opportunity of seeing the game played by two of the best exponents of the present day, but perhaps the inaccessibility of the links had something to do with this. The Broadway course is most beautifully situated from a scenic point of view, but except for those provided with motor cars – or better still, those who have friends who own motors – it is most difficult to reach. The nearest railway station is Willersey halt and from here there is a long dusty climb which is calculated to give even the most enthusiastic devotee of the royal and ancient game reason to pause before undertaking the journey. The writer reached the top of Willersey Hill by this means on Saturday, and though he and his companions felt that they had had almost enough walking to satisfy them for some hours before they joined the players, yet the magnificence of the prospect over the Vale of Evesham and the delight they experienced in watching the game played by two such experts soon dispelled any feeling of weariness and amply repaid the labour of reaching the course.

The writer goes on to comment on the greens, lumpy in places due to the drying winds having made them too hard to roll. His description of the match runs into 14 inches of column space, a feat of observation and detail. Duncan beat Mayo 147 to 152.

Continuing Difficulties

But the German war machine soon was to grind over Europe and blight everything.

Dr. Standring commented at the AGM of 1913 on the most successful year in the club's history. £28 0s 0d had been taken in green fees – but the overall deficit was £14 12s 3d. In spite of all efforts each year saw a deficit – 1914, £33 8s 1d; 1915, £13 1s 9d. The Great War was only obliquely mentioned regarding the continuing deficit: "all things considered it was not to be wondered at" and eventually it was decided to carry on the club but still reduce the wages by employing the groundsman three days a week instead of six for the months of November to March. This would save the club £10!

By 1916 the committee was dubious as to whether the club should be continued due to the financial situation. Having decided to press on, it was agreed to keep the groundsman's hours limited.

By 1917 membership had fallen, both men and ladies.

Lord Elcho disappeared from the list. Having lost his two eldest sons in the war, he was devastated with grief. But at long last the hostilities finished, the influence of new, enthusiastic and possibly younger members of the committee was being felt. The club continued. As might be expected the post-war years once more saw an increase in membership – ten new members in 1919, 22 in 1920.

AN ACCOUNTS MYSTERY

In the minutes of October 1919, it is recorded that Mr. Patten, the hon. treasurer had gone to California and had withdrawn his guarantorship and the bank had closed the account. "It was decided to write to Mr. Patten asking for explanation regarding several items in the accounts." In August, 1920 "It was proposed by the vicar and seconded by Mr. de Navarro that Messrs. Lloyd, Flower and Patten should be held responsible for the overdraft and that the bank account be closed and a new account opened."

On September 16th, 1920 "A letter was read from H. J. Patten and the Secretary was asked to reply stating that the balance sheets were pasted in the minute book and it was open to inspection by Mr. Patten any time and the committee hope he will resolve this matter without delay or appoint an accountant to do so for him." But the last balance sheet pasted in the minute book was 1916–17! The problem had not been resolved by January, 1921, when another letter was sent to the late treasurer asking him to reply, "the answers to his various questions having being furnished".

The mystery remains unsolved, but it is interesting to speculate. At the 27th AGM, the nettle was finally grasped and the subscription was raised for playing members: £3 3s 0d men, £2 2s 0d ladies, £1 1s 0d town members (a new term with no explanation given). By the AGM of 1922 the hon. treasurer was able to report a balance in hand of £30 1s 3d. This improvement was to continue for a few years.

NEW LANDLORD

The turning point in the fortunes of the club was due to several things – the end of the war, an influx of fresh enthusiasm and a new lease.

Since its inception the club had been unable to obtain a lease of more than one year and there was always haggling with both landlord and other tenants, over quite paltry sums of money. The breakthrough came in 1920 when the Farncombe Estates were bought by Captain Alan Butler for his mother and stepfather, Captain and Mrs. Frank Burges. The Burgeses were to be entitled to remain there for their lifetime. Minutes of April, 1920, show that a letter was received from Captain Burges asking for rent of £46 10s and granting the club a lease of seven years. With hindsight, this was a red letter day for the club but they decided to reply and point out that previously, when the club paid £46 10s the landlord paid rates, repair of walls and hedges, and tax. In other words the committee did not grab the opportunity with the keenness which might have been expected. However it is amusing to note that Mr. de Navarro stated he would be pleased to propose Captain Burges as president. It was fortuitous that Mr. Lloyd had withdrawn from the stage leaving the carrot of the presidency to be offered elsewhere. By the

AGM of October, 1920, all was settled; the agreement was signed, Captain Burges was elected a member of the club as well as being elected president. "Carried unanimously".

Over the years Captain Burges was to prove he was not an easy man with whom to do business. An old gentleman who knew him confirmed this impression, rather euphemistically, that he was certainly "difficult".

MORE CHANGE

New lease, new landlord and now new hon. sec. In 1921 Dr. Standring retired from his post and was made captain, a much less onerous duty. On December 23rd, 1921, Mr. de Navarro, as the oldest member of the club, made a presentation to Dr. Standring, a man he called "the Alma Pater of Broadway sport".

With Dr. Alexander as the new incumbent it seems that the club's affairs gained fresh impetus. At the end of 1922 a discussion took place regarding suggested improvements to the course. "C. H. Mayo who was present by invitation outlined a scheme for the alteration of some of the holes. It was decided to leave the matter in the hands of the committee." What a pity the scheme was either not recorded or has been lost. However it is clear that doubts about the 8th were being voiced. "It was proposed that the stone wall at the 1st, 4th and 8th holes be taken down but should it be decided to dispense with the present 8th that wall be left."

New implements were obtained – two iron rollers in 1922 and it was proposed a Triplex mower be purchased in 1923 at a cost of £140. This machine was capable of cutting a 7ft swathe "and would be the means of keeping the course in first class order throughout the year". A new implement shed was a must and Mr. Keyte undertook the erection free of charge. In 1923 the course had been surveyed and the length of the holes determined. Three new bunkers were made on the 9th hole.

NEW PROFESSIONAL

At the 29th AGM 1923 the engagement of a professional was discussed, Dr. Alexander briefly stating the type of man required. On October 27th, 1923, the hon. sec. was instructed to engage a professional for the club "at a

Frank Bisgrove, his first day as Broadway G.C. professional

wage not exceeding £2 per week". He told the committee that he had heard good accounts of F. Bisgrove at Burnham. Frank Bisgrove was duly engaged at a weekly wage of £1 10s to commence duties on February 1st, 1924. He was to stay with the club for 40 years when his job was taken over by John Freeman and in 1992 by his son Martyn. So in a hundred years the club has had only four professionals. Frank Bisgrove learnt his golf at Burnham-on-Sea under Bob Bradbeer, a player well known in golfing circles in the south-west. Miss Jennifer Foxon, our leading lady player for several years, remembers Frank Bisgrove in his later years and she says he was a stylish player who always turned out on a Sunday morning with the men. His dress was not so stylish however as he often wore his wellingtons and a tweed jacket. He was in good company as I am told that the late Mr. Gerald Nabarro MP used to have his golf lessons wearing a pair of green wellingtons!

DEVELOPMENT OF GOLF

The presentation of a trophy by Mr. Lloyd was a stimulus to competition and results were reported keenly from its inception in 1912. Entry for the competition was open to all members, including ladies.
Evesham Journal, March, 1922

Broadway Golf Club
The final tie for the Lloyd Cup, given by a former president in 1919, was played on Wednesday afternoon, between Mr. S. Shovelton (12) and Mr. H. C. Randall (16). After a hard game, Mr. Randall, though the longer-handicapped man, played much the better and won somewhat easily. After the match was over, Madame de Navarro presented the cup to the winner and congratulated him on having come through the competition successfully and jokingly remarked on his living in Moreton-in-Marsh, that as Sir Thomas Lipton said he would try to lift the American Yachting Cup, so someone from Broadway would try to lift the cup back to Broadway next year.

The Kenyon Stow salver continued to be played for as a quarterly medal. In December, 1921, "It was decided to play for the Kenyon Stow Salver on the second Wednesday of February, May, August and November as a perpetual challenge prize for the best Medal Round."

On his retirement from the post of hon. sec. in 1921, Dr. Standring presented a trophy which, with a touch of humour, was to be known as the "Standrinks" Cup. "This was to be played for on the second Saturday of January, April, July and October as a perpetual challenge prize against Bogey." These early members were very keen on perpetuity but as years pass all things become transient and although this old double-handled tankard still stands, albeit on the bottom shelf of the cabinet, hardly any present-day member has heard of it; it was retired in 1978. Open meetings were held. This was one of them.

BROADWAY GOLF CLUB

An Open Meeting will be held on the Broadway course
on Saturday, November 18th, 1921.
1. 18 holes Medal Round (under handicap), for a Tankard presented by Dr. C. T.
Standring, and a 2/6d. sweepstake. Winner taking two thirds; second one third.
2. 18 holes Bogey (handicap). 2/6d. Sweepstake. Winner two thirds of sweepstake;
second one third.
Play to commence at 9.30am.
Lunch (2/6) at the Farm.
Green fee for non-members 2/-.

According to the newspaper, the first event was won by S. B. Walker of Stratford whilst the afternoon was a tie between H. Jones and Dr. Alexander "with 9 down".

A handwritten comment underneath states, "A good deal of snow on the course and greens freezing in the afternoon" – one thing that time cannot change.

In 1923 when Harold Keyte had won the Lloyd Cup and the Standrinks trophy for two quarters in succession, it was to cause some discussion and lead to modification of the rules of the competition so as the same player could not continue winning time after time. But this decision was changed several times.

Broadway joined the Midland Association of Golfers in 1921 and continued to play an increasing number of matches with local clubs like Evesham and Stratford. In February 1924 a match was played against Copt Heath at Broadway – easier communications and transport meant that longer distances could be contemplated.

LADIES

There had been lady members at Broadway since Dr. Standring first brought the game to the village. His wife was certainly a golfer and actually played in the club team in 1894 against Alcester. There is no evidence of whether ladies like Madame de Navarro took an active part in the game. However, by the 1920s the influence of Mrs. Alexander (a Scottish international player) and her daughter was seen and they certainly played golf to a high standard. Miss Alexander (handicap 24) reached the third round of the Lloyd

Miss Peggy Alexander

37

Cup in 1922, only to be beaten in the next round by the eventual winner, H. Randall (handicap 12).

Unlike at many clubs, ladies attended the AGMs and had a say in matters. The AGM of October 25th, 1922 is significant. "It was agreed that ladies are members of the club *on the same standing as men,* except that their subscription is £2 2s 0d instead of £3 3s 0d but that in club competitions all handicaps are limited to 24."

It was proposed that the lady members should appoint a sub-committee amongst themselves to arrange competitions confined to ladies only and to select teams for ladies matches. The committee was chosen, consisting of Mrs. Alexander, Mrs. Arkwright, Miss Ashwin, Mrs. Peirs Duncombe and Miss Scott.

Thus Broadway Golf Club was very democratic in its attitudes, remarkable when one considers the era of the suffragette was recent history and full enfranchisement of women did not take place till 1928.

The matter of a ladies dressing room was considered and eventually agreed upon in January, 1923 "if the money could be raised without touching the club funds". A Mr. Knox offered to provide materials at cost price. A letter was sent out asking for subscriptions; a dance was arranged to raise funds, and eventually the work was done as well as the addition of a men's room.

At a committee meeting on May 28th, 1924 "A letter was read from Mrs. Arkwright, the honorary secretary of the Ladies' Golf Club asking if the club would pay the entrance fee and annual subscription to the Ladies Golf Union." This was agreed. By the 30th AGM the minutes state, "The ladies had joined the Ladies' Golf Union, and it was considered that the prestige gained by this act, and the fact that lady members could now receive a handicap which would exact official recognition on the other courses, would prove a very valuable step in the progress of the club". Unfortunately the early minute books of the ladies section have been lost.

DEATH OF THE FOUNDER

At the 30th AGM on November 22nd, 1924, Mr. de Navarro rose to pay a tribute to the memory of Dr. Standring, the founder of the club who had died on November 8th. He spoke of the irreparable loss the club had sustained by his untimely death. He read out a letter from the Stratford-on-Avon Golf Club expressing their sympathy. Mr. de Navarro proposed that Dr. Standring's name should be retained on the list of members, in perpetuity (that word again) – a proposal which was seconded by Mr. Everett and carried. "It was proposed by Mr. Everett that a cup be provided, out of the club funds, and suitably inscribed to be a permanent and indestructible memorial of the affection and esteem in which Dr. Standring was held by the members of the Broadway Golf Club and to conserve his name to the club for all time." They did not realise that by naming this trophy The Founders' Cup the name of Dr. Standring would not be conserved, even though the "Founder's" as it is known, is one of the major competitions for the men. The trophy itself is considered to be one of the best pieces to be produced by its maker, Mr. George Hart of Chipping Campden, a noted silversmith. Mr. Hart offered to make a replica of the cup for £2 for the winners to keep. The offer was accepted and two replicas ordered but we do not know how long this custom continued.

Thus ended an era. Broadway Golf Club was now entering on a period of modest growth and development but whilst it was still a nine hole course, remote from town or city, it was fated to remain a golfing backwater for some time yet.

Third Period, 1911–24

1911, new nine hole course, Willersey Hill Farm. 75 acres. Leased. Hobley of Cheltenham designed.

1912, new pavilion.

1912, "Village Members", Broadway's artisans, first admitted.

1914, exhibition match between Charles Mayo and George Duncan (later British Open Champion).

1919, Mr. T. H. Lloyd presented Lloyd Cup.

1920, first seven-year lease.

1921, Dr. Standring retires as hon. sec. and replaced by Dr. Alexander.

1921, first Open Meeting.

1924, Frank Bisgrove (professional) engaged.

1924, ladies join LGU for first time.

1924, death of Founder.

Chapter Four

Steady Progress 1924–39

The "Alexandrian" Era

T HE periods into which this history has been divided are by no means arbitrary. In fact this fourth period could well have begun in 1921 when Dr. Alexander took over the reins as hon. sec. and his influence was immediately felt, for example in the employment of a professional. But it is not until after the death of the founder that one can detect a general switch of emphasis. The early members were affected by the insecurity of their leases, the unsuitability of the land they were

Dr. Alexander with his two sons Arthur and Gordon in front of the pavilion 1913. Both boys later had distinguished service careers

able to rent, lack of cash, inaccessibility, small membership. These matters preoccupied the committee, whilst the golf, which was their "raison d'être", seemed almost incidental.

There is no doubt that the acquisition of the seven-year lease in 1920 opened fresh horizons. Longer-term planning could take place and the inaccessibility problem was diminishing with the development of the motor car. Improvements were made to the course, the clubhouse, facilities for the professional and perhaps most importantly they spent more time discussing the game itself and how it should be played at Broadway. However the committee's efforts were not always backed up by the co-operation of members who did not support competitions in spite of increasing numbers.

Dr. William Gordon Alexander

Dr. Alexander joined the club with his wife and first mention of him in the minutes is during the year 1912–1913. However, as the family came to Broadway in 1908 it is safe to assume they started playing immediately as both he and his wife were accomplished players in Scotland. Before the death of the founder in 1924 he had become hon. sec., a position he was to hold from 1921 until November 1932. He was captain twice, in 1929 and 1934–35, and president from 1933 until 1945. Thus he was an influential figure during a very important era for the club when times were difficult after the First World War, during the Depression and to the end of the Second World War. The records leave one in no doubt that on many occasions it was the efforts of Dr. Alexander which kept the wheels turning. When he arrived in the north Cotswolds there were few made-up roads and communications – especially in winter – were difficult. Journeys by trap, on horseback and even a bicycle were the order of the day. He travelled thousands of miles on horseback – probably often using this

Alexander family on the old 1st green (now the 17th)

41

method of transport to go off for his game of golf, hitching up to the rail which was provided in front of the old clubhouse. He became president of the Gloucestershire Golf Union in 1932 and a member of the R. and A. Broadway Golf Club was lucky to have found a man of such personality and vigour to fill Dr. Standring's shoes.

THE COURSE

During the first years of this period care of the course continued in the same way as previously. Nothing spectacular was done, just a small change here, an improvement there. Always money or to be more accurate lack of it, played a very important role. For example in November, 1924, Sir Philip Stott suggested that the bunkers on the farther side of the 3rd green might be sloped rather more gradually, "the present angle being rather in the nature of a penalty when putting under certain circumstances". A forward tee was made for the ladies at the 7th. The grass keep was placed in the hands of Righton and Son, to be let by auction or private tender. In 1925 Captain Burges proposed that the club subscribe £1-1/- annually to the Scientific Advisory Green Committee, R. and A. Golf Club, St. Andrews.

A hint as to the financial position at this time is seen in September, 1927 when it was reported that A. Bowen, greenkeeper since 1921, had resigned due to ill health. It was suggested that the professional take over the green-keeper's job as well (a situation which was to repeat itself several times in later years). A man to work under Bisgrove was needed "his wages not to be more than £1-15/- and the question of Bisgrove's wages to be considered later as it was generally felt that the club could not afford more than £3-10/- per week for the two men".

Meanwhile the lease was due for renewal and a sum of £55 per annum was agreed with Captain Burges's solicitor. The security of tenure for seven years with an option on the next seven years was appreciated.

The club was a little more affluent by February, 1929 because the committee were considering the purchase of either a new horse and sets of harness or a motor tractor. Advice was sought from the secretaries of Stinchcombe and Tadmarton regarding a Metropolitan Tractor at £125. A Fordson would cost £200. After a demonstration, Mr. New, Broadway Garage, was "instructed to buy a Metropolitan Tractor, Type A with a Tip Cart attachment". They bought a Ransomes "Certes" mowing machine for the greens. Thus Broadway Golf Club entered the mechanised world.

The letting of the grazing was abandoned at this time "the disadvantages of having sheep on the course outweighed the small amount of revenue received".

The Course in the 1920s

4th green

5th green

The Course in the 1920s

6th green

7th green

PLANS FOR MORE MAJOR IMPROVEMENT

By September 24th, 1929, the money in hand was £150 on deposit and £112 in the current account, with very few outstanding accounts and it was therefore agreed that £150 be spent on improving the course. The hon. sec. was instructed to contact Dr. Mackenzie, golf architect, regarding the expense of a personal visit.

Dr. Mackenzie's work on three world famous courses brought him lasting fame – Cypress Point and Augusta National in the USA and the Royal Melbourne in Australia. The most famous hole in his designs is the 16th at Cypress Point, a par 3, with a carry of 200 yards over the Pacific. And it was this man whose advice was sought by the committee of Broadway Golf Club.

In October, 1929, he replied stating his fee for a visit and design for a new green would be twenty guineas, a sum which the committee decided was beyond the means of the club. By November he had changed his mind and offered to come for £5-5/-, plus first-class travel. This was accepted.

Dr. Mackenzie visited on November 28th, 1929. At the December committee meeting the secretary read "a very full report on the course ... with suggestions for improvements and advice as to future upkeep. This report was much appreciated by the committee ... and it was unanimously decided to proceed with reconstruction of the 4th green and the making of a new 2nd green." Some years later, at the club's annual dinner on December 8th, 1951, Mr. Rayner Booth stated that "Dr. Alexander designed the 5th green from a nettle bed. Dr. Mackenzie (well-known golf designer) designed the 3rd, Tom Simpson the 8th, and the present professional, F. Bisgrove and Mr. Booth himself the 7th. The rest were just the fairway."

However, back to 1929, when "the secretary was instructed to ask Dr. Mackenzie to send a skilled foreman to superintend the work at £4 a week and to engage labourers at 6/- a day to carry out the work".

Discussion on the new 8th hole was postponed till a better idea was obtained of money available; by February 25th, 1930 £125 had been spent. It would have been too much to hope that this report was still in existence after all these years.

By 1931 the club was employing Bisgrove at £3 10s 0d, a tractor driver at 35/- and a groundsman at 32/6d per week.

CUTHBERT RAYNER BOOTH

The influence of Mr. Booth in Broadway Golf Club cannot be exaggerated. He became a playing member in the mid 1920s, was elected to the committee at the 36th AGM in 1930 and hon. sec. at the 38th AGM in 1932. Thus began an association which was to prove long and interesting. An athlete in his young days, he had been a student at Wadham College, Oxford. He played rugger and rowed for his college and became a boxing blue. During the First World War he was an observer in the Royal Flying Corps. After coming to the Cotswolds he took an active part in local life – councillor on North Cotswold RDC, governor of Campden Grammar School, wing commander in the Air Training Corps. The reputation that has survived is that he was an autocrat. The style of the minutes bears this out, reflecting the character of each hon. sec., progressing from sparse with Dr. Standring, adequate with Dr. Alexander, to pedantic and lengthy to the n'th degree with Mr. Booth, especially when he decided to use a typewriter.

This must necessarily affect the information which can be gleaned from the minutes. How far are they affected by the person writing them even though countersigned by someone else? This seems especially pertinent with Mr. Booth. He was allowed a great deal of latitude because in spite of his authoritative style of management, he was a willing worker who enjoyed organising and then as ever, it was not easy to find people to fill onerous, honorary positions (as Dr. Alexander found in 1930 when his appeal for assistance fell on deaf ears). He was to cross many people, including Dr. Alexander, during his tenure. At the AGM in 1937 he proposed a sincere vote of thanks to the hon. sec. "with whom I so often begged to differ". Probably Mr. Booth mellowed a little in his old age when a comment in the minutes of the AGM in 1954 reads "the hon. sec. has been more amenable of late". The following few paragraphs are typical of Mr. Booth's style of management.

BATTLE IS ENGAGED

Several closely typed pages in the records beginning September 25th, 1934 are filled with details of a feud which was developing between Mr. Booth and a Mr. P. O. Heatherley. Mr. Heatherley is still alive in his nineties and was pleased and amused to explain. A special meeting was called to investigate a claim from a Mr. Clark concerning Mr. Heatherley's behaviour towards him. Letters went to and fro which Mr. Booth alleged contained attacks on himself. He insisted on going through the whole of these letters. The tenor of the meeting can be surmised from the following: "Capt. Napier rose on a point of order and asked if it was necessary to go through all this." On being told yes "Capt. Napier said he had a train to meet and promptly left the room". Asked recently what he had said (because of course Mr. Booth kept it out of the minutes) Mr. Heatherley said he had called Mr. Clark and Mr. Booth "pot hunters". Deeply offended the hon. sec. resigned (the first of many times) adding there had been "certain unprovoked attacks on him in the suggestion book".

Of course Mr. Booth was persuaded to stay on. But this was not the end of Mr. Heatherley. On March 16th, 1935 "Behaviour of a Member" the secretary read a letter he had written the chairman concerning the behaviour of Mr. Heatherley towards himself. His subs were six months overdue, when asked to pay he used "strong language stating he not only had deliberately held up his payment but that he would pay when he … chose". Asked to leave, Mr. Heatherley promptly joined Evesham Golf Club. Imagine the electric atmosphere when these two were drawn together in a match shortly after. Mr. Heatherley says he won 8 and 7! The quarrel was patched up some time later when they met accidentally in Chipping Campden. They shook hands and Mr. Heatherley re-entered the Broadway fold and when the new nine holes were made in 1962 was delighted to be in charge of making the new greens for no other reason than that he had the best lawn in Chipping Campden. This is according to Jack Gorin, still a playing member in his eighties, who was captain at the time.

A Quiet Couple of Years

1931 and 1932 were uneventful as far as the course was concerned. It was proposed that it should be played as 18 holes by means of extra tees but this was not thought practical. Discussion regarding a new 8th green continued. Bearing in mind what the 8th was like at this time one would have expected that it should have been a priority. As far as greens in general were concerned it was decided "the chief item under this head was worms". A 12" mowing machine was bought for the greens and in January 1933 "2 Patisson tractors, one of latest type were purchased from Lillybrook Golf Club for £32/10-". Sufficient money was saved in this transaction for a compost shed to be afforded and a shed to house the extra tractor. However it was later reported that repair bills for these tractors ate up the saving.

New Water Scheme

Sir Philip Stott, club captain 1925–26, by profession an architect, had devised a scheme for supplying water to the greens. A study of the local Ordnance Survey map shows the hillside to have several springs and in fact water still constantly runs down Willersey Hill road in all weathers. In January, 1933 the volume of water from the springs was gauged over a period. There were three under consideration. One was Gunn's spring, which gave an uneven output and was very sensitive to rainfall. It varied between 100 gallons per hour after rain to 48 gallons normal. Ingle's spring proved difficult to gauge and showed variation due to house use as well as rainfall. The best was in the rough paddock (below the 6th). This showed no appreciable variation from 225/250 gallons per hour. "Both for position and supply this latter was definitely the best". Bomford and Evershed were approached for advice and possible contract. On February 11th, 1933, it was resolved to lay water to a tank above the clubhouse and connect up as many greens as possible. The water was to be driven up to the tank by a wind pump then gravity fed through iron pipes to the greens. Some of these pipes still remain. Captain Burges was to be approached with a view to his putting in the scheme and charging rent. Failing this, the club would carry out the scheme as far as possible. A part scheme would cost £125 and a whole scheme £200 if direct labour was used; contract labour would cost considerably more.

Unfortunately Captain Burges objected to a windmill pump as being unsightly, but by March 1933 he had given his permission to use water from Gunn's corner (that is the crossroads at the top of Willersey Hill) and he removed his embargo on the pump, therefore the club decided to go ahead with the whole scheme. The ruins of the wind pump could until recently be found below the 8th tee.

The money was raised by means of guarantors of £10 and £20, the hon. sec. and treasurer being left to obtain as many guarantors as possible. The water scheme was eventually completed at "considerably less than expected and had, during the long dry spell of weather (summer 1933) been of incalculably benefit to the club. The greens were kept so that it had been possible to putt on them in direct contrast to some of the neighbouring courses". Acting on the advice of the Board of Green Keeping Research the hon. sec. had "dressed the greens constantly during the season which he felt would improve them during the coming winter season". In March 1935 Mr. Booth commissioned a book on the course and "he was so pleased with the original drawings that he had obtained these drawings for hanging in the clubhouse". These same drawings now hang in the new clubhouse at the end of the casual bar and show many interesting old features. Look carefully and it is possible to see the early club hut which was taken over by the village players, and also the old wind pump.

Hole 1, 357 yards, The Approach

Hole 2, 271 yards, The Approach with quarry on left

Hole 3, 415 yards

Hole 4, 487 yards

Hole 5, 145 yards, The Drive

Hole 6, 350 yards

Hole 7, 298 yards, The Drive

The Blind 8th, 122 yards, The Old Hole

52

Hole 9, 365 yards, The Drive

MORE CHANGES ON THE COURSE

This same year another notable golf architect was consulted, namely Tom Simpson. Amongst his work was the design of Royal Antwerp, Club du Lys, Chantilly, Paris. The committee at Broadway had certainly widened their sights from the days when they called in Mr. Hobley of Cheltenham. By September Mr. Simpson had visited the course and laid out a plan for the 8th hole, the 9th green and alteration to the 7th. By the beginning of 1936 several banks had been removed on the right-hand side of the first fairway as well as on the left-hand side of the third. The position of a new green on the 9th was to be determined by testing out several different places after further banks had been removed.

When Mr. Simpson revisited he declared himself so pleased with the situation and general layout that Mr. Booth reported, "He has designed a new 8th hole which the committee are at the moment carrying out and I feel this will be a vast improvement to the course." How right he was – by the following February the committee expressed their pleasure at the layout of the 8th, no doubt relieved to be rid of the high shot off the tee over the top of the bank.

Regarding the new 9th green it was decided to put up a notice for a meeting suggesting it to be put into play for three months for members to formulate opinions, after which a General Meeting should be called to decide whether it be completed with the necessary guarding bunkers, as designed by Mr. Simpson, and continued as the 9th green, or be scrapped and the existing remain. However, Bisgrove made an error and put it into play immediately "in spite of the fact that it was being dressed and not fit to play on". On November 14th, 1936 it was given the thumbs down by the members in favour of the old green, the new one to be used for practising. It has not been possible to establish whether this green is the one still in use for practising by the present 1st tee.

The plans of Mr. Simpson for the 7th green were finally completed by the end of 1937. It had been moved forward bodily to a fresh spot. It played well and was considered to be a great improvement to the hole.

In 1938 the old pavilion by the 5th was emptied and left open for shelter for players. Some members still walked up to the club along the footpath across the old 1901 course.

WAGES

Agricultural wages had risen some 2/- during 1935 and at a meeting held after the AGM November 1936, it was agreed to raise the wages of the three permanent staff by 2/- a week, from the week commencing October 1st, 1936. The staff was not totally satisfied with this and a circular went to members.

I have had a request for a rise in wages paid to our staff. Owing to the increase in Agricultural Wages to 32/- and to the roadmen of the county to 40/- and 42/- casual the Committee voluntarily last November raised all wages by 2/-. This gave Bisgrove 42/-, Ernest 37/-, Reginald 35/- (the Foulkes brothers) and casual 33/-. The deductions for insurance and unemployment are a big item now, being 1/7d per week and rent, insurance, unemployment, club amount to roughly 10/- per week. This request comes at an awkward time for me as I intended asking that the permanent staff should be continued at three men, as I cannot keep the course in proper order with only two.

The committee agreed to an increase in permanent staff as well as an increase of a further 2/- to Ernest and Reginald making them 39/- and 37/- respectively. They were to try to obtain an extra labourer at 32/- a week. Bisgrove missed out on this occasion, which seems rather mean, as he was employed "under different terms". He remained only 3/- more than the groundsman! High wages being offered at the Aeroplane Works in 1937 were making it very difficult to find and keep labour. Mr. Booth was given a free hand on wages so that he could keep his staff.

The alterations to the course had needed extra labour to be employed to the extent of £100. This upset the regular staff and culminated in Reginald Foulkes handing in his notice. The hon. sec. decided to manage without another man.

LADIES

At the beginning of the period 1924–38 the ladies continued for the time being to take an active part in the affairs of Broadway Golf Club. They were fairly well represented at the AGMs, considering the disproportionate numbers of male and female members. However, whilst the ladies were in a more favourable position than in many clubs, it is obvious they were still expected to take the traditional female role of producers of refreshment.

"10th, Nov. 1926 – Mr. Jones proposed a vote of thanks to ladies who under the leadership of Mrs. Harbidge, had provided tea on match days and spoke in eulogistic terms of the fare provided". Dr. Alexander then suggested that more ladies help as the work had fallen on three or four only (a familiar situation). Profit from the teas arranged by Miss Alexander had provided crockery and furniture for the new extension and they still had £5 in hand. By 1936 the enthusiasm of the ladies for acting as unpaid caterers had waned and Dr. Alexander is mentioning difficulty in expecting voluntary work. Mrs. Bowen, who already worked at his house, Pond Close, was asked to take over the job.

The Alexander ladies were the keen golfers of the section. In 1925 "A mixed tournament was proposed by Mrs. Alexander and agreed", One of the leading lady golfers of the day, Miss Cecilia Leitch, played a match at Broadway in 1925 and complimented the club on the good order of the course. Miss Leitch became a multiple champion of Britain, France and once of Canada.

In 1929 ladies were still eligible to enter club competitions and could play on their LGU handicaps plus three. However by 1931 it was proposed by Guy Pemberton that "Ladies' and men's competitions shall be separate and that the ladies manage their section of the club as distinct from the men's". Finally a decision at the AGM 1931, meant competitions for the Lloyd, Founders and Standrinks trophies as well as the monthly medal were to be confined to men and ladies should have their own competitions. Two years later this was amended to allow ladies with LGU handicaps to compete for the monthly medal cup but no handicap over 24 be recognised.

Ladies meeting at Cleeve Hill 1920s. Peggy and Mrs. Alexander are standing 2nd and 4th from left

The ladies' team at this time was fairly successful, due largely to the skill of Miss Peggy Alexander, winning 50 per cent of their matches, a slightly better average than the men.

1930 was a notable year for the ladies in another direction, in that the secretary of the Ladies Club became an ex officio member of the general committee. The first lady to take her place was Miss Douglas Jones, of The Hill, Broadway. The ladies were being encouraged to be more independent. But by November, 1935, Mr. Booth was reporting "Ladies have made some progress during the year, but not as much as I should have liked and I am anxious that a greater interest should be shown by them in club matters." The match results of this season were poor, played 6, won 1, halved 1, lost 4 and 5 other matches which had been arranged were scratched.

The following year a request from the ladies committee for mixed foursomes on Easter Sunday was refused. "Until the number of handicaps in the ladies' section is considerably increased, it is impossible to arrange for mixed foursomes to be played". This refusal, surprisingly, was from Dr. Alexander.

Improvement was seen the following year (not in match success however: played 10, won 3, lost 7).

The ladies section has worked better this year under the able secretaryship of Mrs. Baber, and this section looks like being a strong one in the future.

This was the comment of Mr. Booth but by the AGM in 1937 he had changed his mind saying:

"I regret to report that this season has proved a complete failure and fiasco. The interest taken in the Club by the ladies is absolutely nil. For a General Meeting (of ladies) 75 invitations were sent out and 3 attended. For matches 18 to 20 cards have to be sent out and then the team is often short, as members who have promised to play fail to turn up, or having not troubled to reply, turn up and are annoyed there is no room for them. The loss to the ladies teas is such that I have been compelled to disassociate the club from these and in the event of no teas being provided for matches, there will I fear, be no matches. Mrs. Baber as hon. sec. has struggled manfully against the rot. In all other matters I am able to act and as members of the club, ladies have equal rights with the men, and their complaints if any, will receive the same attention."

As a former boxing blue Mr. Booth did not pull his punches.

The ladies had received some consideration regarding the comfort of their room, which they complained was cold, cheerless and uncomfortable and as their membership was now over 80 the secretary thought their complaint justified. "The committee agreed that a stove, carpet, table and looking glass be obtained, provided that the cost was not over £10."

So the ladies section went into decline for some years until revived in the 1950s.

SURPRISING GOLFING APATHY

Monthly medals continued to be played. The main trophy had been the Lloyd Cup but was now joined by the Founder's Cup. At a committee meeting on January 17th, 1925 "It was decided that £21 having been collected for a Standring Memorial Prize, the competition should be played under the following conditions. Qualifying Medal round of 18 holes under handicap to be played on the first Saturday in October. The first eight in the qualifying round to play off by match play, 18 hole matches, under handicap the following week. The final to be played on the second Saturday in

October." The prize was to be called "The Founder's Cup in memory of Dr. Standring". As time went on, the last few words disappeared. The following year it was suggested that in order that the replicas be distributed among members as much as possible, no member may hold the cup more than once in three years. The two replicas have disappeared. Possibly they remained on someone's mantelpiece somewhere in Broadway. Entry for the competition was not good so this notion was abandoned and by November 1927, the period of play was extended to encourage more players – only 19 entries had been received. In 1934 it was all change again when it was thought that dispensing with the eliminating rounds would persuade more members to play, so the Founder's was played over 36 holes, the same as the Lloyd in those days.

In 1931 play for the Kenyon Stowe salver was abandoned and it was to be kept on show in the case. Yet in spite of the apparent apathy towards competitions, in January, 1935 Dr. Alexander presented The Alexander Cup for competition among members. This was a knockout competition, foursomes, under handicap. Another cup was presented by the club in 1936 to be competed for by members who had beaten Bisgrove playing off scratch. Bisgrove received a fee of 2/6d per match but due to lack of support, the Standrinks Bogey Cup was withdrawn in May, 1937. (Later this double handled pewter tankard was used as the prize for the Lloyd Plate, Keith Gilbert being the last person to win it, in 1978, after which it was abandoned in one of the periodical attempts to streamline the number of competitions.)

At the AGM of 1937 Mr. Booth commented "Competitions have not been supported as well as I should like, the Standrinks Bogey Cup was withdrawn principally owing to the indifferent support shown, and the regular monthly medals are not very good. Members turn out well if reminded by card on each occasion, but the expense and consumption of my time makes this impossible to carry out."

At this time also, the Junior Cup was abandoned. This was not a trophy for youngsters, but for beginners at the game.

From time to time a charity match would be played, for example in aid of the new Shakespeare Memorial Theatre at the request of Stratford-on-Avon Golf Club, summer 1927. This took the form of a running bogey competition in which ladies were allowed to play on LGU handicap plus six strokes. In 1937 they held a competition in aid of the Guide Dogs – the hon. sec. promised to "take the hat round" to raise £5 for a cup.

Over the years one or two ideas were tried to encourage interest. Special afternoons were arranged for meeting to fix up matches. Bisgrove tried drawing partners for the monthly medal to introduce change around. All failed.

GLOUCESTERSHIRE COUNTY GOLF UNION

In 1925 the club had been given representation on the Gloucestershire County Golf Union. In return the County Union Executive was invited to hold a competition at Broadway on May 3rd.

At the AGM in 1930 it was proudly announced that the Gloucester County Championship had been won by a member of the club, a Mr. H. P. Bazely with scores of 72 and 73 = 145, under extremely difficult conditions. Six other members had competed. However, requests to the Gloucestershire County Union failed to trace Mr. Bazely from Broadway. Search in the contemporary *Gloucester Echo* revealed "Gloucestershire County Meeting at Cleeve Hill – Cheltenham Club's Success …

THE WINNING CARD Bazeley's winning round of 72 contained no figure over 5 but we think the player had already achieved that feat and so won the box of balls which is offered for its performance.

The full list of leading scores contained no mention of any Broadway member. It was common for top amateur players to be a member of several clubs and the Cheltenham Club, feeling its superiority, managed to claim Mr. Bazeley over Broadway.

PROFESSIONALS

The importance of the golf club professional had increased although the pay was still not high. Broadway was no exception. In September 1926, Bisgrove was given ten days' holiday in October, to enable him to play in a tournament at Burnham. Success would be a good publicity exercise. The committee agreed that £6 per year expenses should be given to Bisgrove to play in the Gloucester Somerset Alliance matches to which Broadway now belonged. A match was held at Broadway on June 18th, 1931, for which a fund of £30 was raised from members.

The *Gloucester Echo* described the match: "There were 17 entries and in spite of the rain and wind some good golf was seen." The winner was A. F. Parker of Cotswold Hills with a total of 148 for two rounds. Bisgrove was last but one with 163.

IMPROVING THE CLUBHOUSE FACILITIES

Committee meetings were not held on a regular basis. There would be several in monthly succession and then a gap of say four months. The habit of meetings at home was dropped and they were held either in the clubhouse during summer months or at the Lygon Arms in the Russell Room, in winter (for obvious reasons I think). This room was used free of charge.

The clubhouse could only be described as very modest and was to remain

On the first tee. Frank Bisgrove, second from left, with unknown players in the 1920s

so for some years in spite of extensions and re-decoration. The club was fortunate in being able to call upon the services of Sir Philip Stott in all building matters. In 1923 a ladies' room and men's room had been added. By 1924 it was realised that Bisgrove needed better premises. Mr. Jones the carpenter, who put up the original building in 1912 (20' x 12' – cost £31 10s) quoted £40 for a shop 18' x 10' x 8' high. This building lasted until 1937 when improvements became necessary as it had started to let in the rain.

By 1927 lockers with keys were available.

Discussion took place in 1929 regarding improvements to the clubhouse which were carried out by Espleys in 1930 at a cost of £138. Unfortunately there is no direct evidence of what these changes were. However, there is mention of a verandah to which a floor was to be added when more funds became available. In the same edition of the *Gloucester Echo* 1930 as the success of Mr. Bazeley was reported there is mention of:

Broadway Mixed Foursomes – The weather was perfect and fourteen couples competed. The entry money went towards a loggia for the club and the prizes were given by Mrs. Hannay and Miss Morgan. A shelter for caddies was to be built whilst changes were in hand. On May 2nd, 1931 a Committee Meeting was held at the clubhouse for the first time in the new room.

In 1932 the clubhouse was to be painted which Mr. Keyte, the local decorator, promised to do at cost. We know that it was heated because in April, 1932, Mr. Booth proposed that a door be put on the caddies' shelter so as it could be used to store coal! Comfort of members had been enhanced back in July 1925, when a licence to sell alcoholic drinks on the club premises was applied for and granted. The management of the bar was placed in the hands of a sub committee, but this arrangement was changed after a couple of years when the drinks were put under the control of the whole committee. One wonders why. In fact the bar was to become a headache for some time to come. The price of drinks was lowered about the same time – beer 8d, whisky and soda 1/8d, small whisky and soda 10d, gin 1/8d, small gin 10d, ginger beer 4d. To add to the luxury, whilst they sipped their drink, members would now be able to read Golf Illustrated which the club had agreed to take. The club was, of course, subject to the licensing laws which were in force at the time – 11am to 2pm and 4pm to 8pm on weekdays and 12 noon to 2pm and 6pm to 9pm on Sundays. It was agreed that the profits on sale of drinks be divided equally between the club and Bisgrove.

A compost shed 30' x 10', an open ended shed of sleepers, weather boards and corrugated iron was bought by the hon. sec. for £16 in 1933. Mr. Booth had started taking things into his own hands "the Sec. thought this amazingly cheap he took it upon himself to agree". This was to cause complaints from the committee in the future.

During this same year a board was put up in the club "with names and dates of the captains since the re-opening after the war". This statement is interesting because there is no evidence that it had ever closed. Finally a phone was installed in 1936.

FINANCE AND MEMBERSHIP

Before the First World War membership stood at around 60 (all types). As might be expected the number dwindled until by 1917 there were about 38 – roughly the same number as 15 years previously. No balance sheet is available for the years between 1918 and 1926 but the few handwritten details in the minutes give a good indication of the improvement in the club's finances after this date which show steady progress except for one or two hiccoughs which are explained by circumstances beyond anyone's control. For example in 1932 there was a drop in membership fees "a falling off due to the continuance of the crisis", suggested Mr. Booth. The crisis mentioned was the effect of the Great Depression and the instability caused by the National Government which was still in power. Weather could also take its toll on income. For example, a fall in green fees (which earlier had been raised from 2/- to 2/6d) in 1932 was blamed on a wet Bank Holiday and in 1933 the very hot weather. Generally speaking the club was on a much sounder financial footing after 1930 when a debit balance of £8 16s 3d changed to a credit balance of £15 2s 1d.

During these years money was being put into a depreciation account and in 1937 it was decided to create a reserve fund from what was previously a deposit account. Back in 1928 an entrance fee of £1 1s 0d had been introduced for the first time and it was decided to add this entrance money to the reserve fund each year. The first investment from this fund was to be Imperial Tobacco, as proposed by Dr. Alexander.

INCREASING NUMBERS

Figures showing the increase in membership are in the minutes of the AGM of 1936:
1933 – 211   1934 – 226   1935 – 217   1936 – 237
The hon. sec. commented in 1936 that membership was increasing "in spite of the opening of a new club at Burford". By 1937 numbers had been augmented again by 20 although Mr. Booth wondered whether a drop in green fees could be blamed on the Coronation!

In June 1938 the treasurer was able to give the following short statement of accounts:

Balance	£332	up	£150
Subs	£462	up	£26
Entrance fees	£32	up	£8
Green fees	£146	up	£33

ADMINISTRATION

As the size of the club increased then Administration had to become more efficient. In the 1920s definite parameters were laid down. The hon. sec. still played the most important role but in 1927 it was agreed that the committee should not consist of more than 13 members including the president, treasurer, captain and secretary. This was elaborated two years later when it was agreed that three senior committee members resign each year but be eligible for re-election. Also Mrs. Alexander proposed that the hon. sec. of the ladies club be ex officio member of the general committee.

At the AGM November 19th, 1930 the position was clarified further "The management of the club shall be in the hands of a general committee which shall consist of the president, captain, secretary and treasurer, who shall be ex officio members and seven members elected at the AGM of the club, four to form a quorum. The three senior members of the committee shall retire each year and not be eligible for re-election till a year had elapsed". Another two years on this was changed again to "two members retire and no radius member to serve on the committee until or unless he has paid a full member's subscription". (The term "radius member" is what we would now call "country member".)

SUBSCRIPTIONS

Although subscriptions were not high the secretary always had difficulty in collecting them. A rule was formulated in 1935 stating, "Any member, after first day of January in any year, who is in arrears with his subscription, cannot use the club for any purpose whatever until such subscription has been paid. That a list of such defaulters be posted in the Club House and that a reminder containing this rule, be sent to all in default." This aspect of administration greatly added to the load of the hon. sec. and treasurer who, in view of the large amount of work done by both, were made honorary members for the duration of their office.

In 1929 Captain Burges resigned the presidency and Mr. de Navarro, a member since the founding of the club, was proposed and Mr. Keyte as captain. This was an important sociological step as Mr. Keyte was a local tradesman, whereas in earlier days prominent social position was a prerequisite of office.

At the same time Mr. Jones, the carpenter, resigned and was made an honorary member for life. The same honour was eventually bestowed on Mr. Keyte when he resigned in 1936 "in view of his length of membership and work he had put in".

Mr. de Navarro died in 1932 leaving the presidency open for Dr. Alexander, the first president to continue to take a very active role in the club instead of being a mere figurehead. At his election "the work done by Dr. Alexander in not only saving the club from being closed down, but in making a really first class course it is at present", was commented on. He also was elected an honorary life member.

1938 – EXCITING TIMES

The club had continued changing gradually. The course had been improved, the clubhouse extended, membership had risen, the financial situation had become more sound. Obviously a point had been reached when the whole structure had to be looked at to meet the new demands. Reading the records of the time, one feels that the committee were quite aware of this but it was an external influence which precipitated change and gave Broadway Golf Club the opportunity to become what it is today, although two or three times the "powers that be" on the committee almost let the chance slip through their fingers.

On October 29th, 1938, a special General Meeting was called at the Lifford Hall, Broadway. Mr. Booth read out the following notice:

On Sundays and Holidays especially, the course gets very crowded and as the membership of the club gradually increases, it has been very evident for some time that some alteration was necessary. This alteration can take two forms, limiting the number of members admitted to the club and raising the green fees or increasing the size of the course by adding nine more holes. Our situation is quite unique, and we have derived a considerable income simply from our view and our altitude, which in the event of our increasing the number of holes will be of great assistance in making the club a still greater success.

The club had been unable to obtain a lease for more than seven years prior to this date but now, for a reason which remains unknown, they had been offered a lease of 21 years on the whole of Willersey Hill Farm, namely 170 acres with an option to purchase at valuation some time in the future.

This acreage consisted of all the land which is the present 18 holes, plus the area extending from the road which runs alongside the present 12th as far as the picnic area, including the farmhouse and yard, as well as the 6 acre field below the 6th.

Captain and Mrs. Burges had only a life interest in the property and as they were by this time becoming elderly, one can speculate that the real owner, Captain Butler, thought it best to ensure continuity before the death of either his mother or stepfather.

The resolution was passed with a strong majority and a special committee was duly appointed to deal entirely with the matter. In fact the general committee were totally preoccupied with the decision. Everything else was definitely put on the back burner. Contemplating a scheme of this nature there were several problems to address. The land they needed for the extra nine holes and the house were tenanted by a Mr. Cotterill (uncle to a present member, Mr. Peter Hartwell, past captain and president). This farmer would have to move. Surplus land, namely the acreage beyond the present 12th and the house, when vacated, would have to be sublet. The farmhouse needed repair work and capital had to be arranged.

Eventually the committee agreed that the maximum sum to be paid in rent for the extra land plus the house and present golf links should be £150.

ADVICE OF EXPERTS

Before business could proceed further, expert opinion had to be sought as to the suitability of the land for a further nine holes and to this end the captain, Captain Ogilvy, Dr. Alexander and Mr. Booth met James Braid of Walton Heath. In his early years James Braid, a Scot, had been an impressive golfer, making golfing history by becoming the first man to win the British Open five times (in nine years) and winning four British Matchplay Championships. As did many of these top-class professionals, he moved on in his later years to golf course design. By the time the committee at Broadway requested his services, he was 68 and the "top nine" was among the last of his plans. His account for the work is recorded as £8 19s 6d.

The greens committee met James Braid on November 18th, 1938. It turned out to be a very foggy day which seriously hampered the inspection of the ground but Braid expressed the view "that if two new holes were made on the present nine hole course, there would be no difficulty in making a very good job of the eighteen holes". He undertook to supply a plan which, when it arrived, the committee were not satisfied that it was a suitable lay-out for the club. No specific details are given and Braid's actual plan has disappeared but the minutes state,

The design and bunkering of the greens being of paramount importance, the committee decided to call in J. H. Turner of Frilford Heath (this being nearer and more convenient) to ascertain as to the probable cost of Braid's lay-out and his fee for superintending the work. Turner suggested several alterations to Braid's plan and to a large extent removed the committee's objections. He followed up with an approximate cost of making all nine new holes at once, and alternatively making them by degrees, and playing on them while in the process of making. This latter being very much cheaper – £450 to £900.

Turner's account, shown later, was three guineas.

PLAN FOR THE COURSE

At the AGM which was held in February, 1939 (not the usual November), the hon. sec. informed members of James Braid's scheme. He had been impressed by the position, contours and turf. However, the committee felt that £900 was too much to spend at once. Turner's idea was to make the new greens in the same way as the existing greens had been made, by rolling out

---

BROADWAY GOLF CLUB

To the Members :

February, 1939.

Your Committee, having obtained James Braid's opinion that a first-class eighteen-hole Course can be made, with the land now available, and the General Meeting, held on February 11th, having resolved to enlarge the present Course to eighteen holes, WE, the Special Committee, are asked to ascertain from Members to what extent they are prepared to support this Scheme.

Although during the last few years it has been possible to build up a substantial Reserve Fund, this Fund is considered insufficient for carrying out the new work necessary, and in addition it is felt that this reserve should not be used for this purpose.

The expenses which have to be met are for making the new holes, compensating the present tenant, seeding down the arable alongside the present 1st fairway, improving our club house accommodation, and provision of accommodation for the Professional's Shop and Shelter for Caddies. It is hoped that it will be possible to make a Club House worthy of a first-class course, standing as it does in such a unique position, which is in itself a very powerful attraction. By the agreement with Capt. Burges, we not only acquire extra land, but also Willersey Hill Farm House and Buildings. Your Committee propose to turn the Farm House into a Guest House, and Dormy House, for the Club, where meals and refreshments can be obtained, to convert some of the buildings into changing rooms, with hot and cold water, a professional's shop, caddies' shelter, etc., with a good draw-in and covered car park. Complete plans with actual estimates will be available very shortly.

In putting forward this scheme your Committee feel confident that it will be more satisfactory than the expedient of spending money on the existing Club House.

It is proposed to issue Debentures of the value of £5 (Five pounds) each, vested in Trustees, with the object of attracting as many of the members as possible. Each year a certain number of Debentures will be drawn, the holders of which will receive £6 for each £5 Debenture drawn, and so arranged that at the end of our lease, the whole of the issue will have been redeemed.

In asking for the sum of £1,500, your Committee feel that this will enable the Club to proceed with the whole scheme, and have the course and club house ready for use early in 1940.

The upkeep cost of the larger course have been carefully considered, and your Committee is of the opinion that this can be maintained efficiently and a sufficient balance be provided for the redemption of the debentures, without any large influx of new members, by the nominal increase in the subscriptions already suggested in the previous circular.

Your Committee also recommend that in the event of any subscriber moving out of the district, permanently, or being unable to participate in the playing of golf for any serious reason, his or her debenture should be paid out, at par, upon request.

A General Meeting will be called directly the Committee are in possession of the information as to what money will be subscribed, then all plans and suggestions will be placed before you, and a decision will be come to as to how the money shall be spent.

A slip is enclosed with this, and we hope that you will make use of it to state the amount which you are prepared to subscribe for.

A stamped addressed envelope is enclosed for your reply.

For the Committee,

C. RAYNER BOOTH,

Hon. Secretary.

existing turf, adding bunkers gradually, as by play the run of the green was discovered. This scheme had the extra appeal of being cheaper – £575, which included the cost of the seeding of the arable. The hope was that this would enable the majority of the holes to be brought into play sooner.

BUILDINGS

First thoughts were that the present clubhouse should remain, altered and enlarged to suit the needs of an 18-hole course. A plan showed improved ladies' quarters, a central canteen, a tea room, an enlarged club room, new men's locker and changing room with modern sanitation throughout. The plan was drawn up by Guy Pemberton, now an architect – estimated cost £250. The club would have the farm house to sublet and they proposed that any tenant should provide meals for golfers "it would serve as a Dormy House and Guest House, and would bring visitors to the club". Plans were also in mind for using out buildings for storage and a large barn for a social club – estimated cost £450.

Quite an ambitious scheme for which money had to be found.

The "collection of sheds" which served as a clubhouse up to 1966

HOW TO RAISE MONEY?

At the AGM on February 11th, 1939, the committee recommended that a private limited company be formed with a capital of £2,000, shares of £5 each to be offered to members, one per member, and in the event of not all being subscribed, the balance required be divided among existing subscribers. Fortunately this scheme was never implemented. What could have happened if the committee had decided to go ahead? If a shareholder died or moved away, the shares could have been sold and it would have been possible for one person or a small group to gain control over all the shares, hence the assets of the club, so in a position to sell out totally if they wished. One or two local clubs did get themselves into this position, so that in modern times the control of the club is in the hands of a board of directors not elected by members. At this same meeting, after lengthy discussion the following proposition was put forward by Mr. Gardiner, seconded by Mr. G. E. Knight, "That the Course be extended to 18 holes as suggested, that the Committee take the necessary steps to raise the money required, and that agreement be entered into with Captain Burges and Captain Butler on terms stated".

Now instead of the limited liability company, Mr. Knight explained another scheme of raising money by redeemable debentures, no doubt realising the pitfalls of the original notion.

In order to be able to borrow money by the issue of debentures a limited company must be formed, not to raise money by the sale of shares but limited by guarantee – in case of need all members had to guarantee the sum of say 10/-, no money changed hands, no share certificates would be given, no dividend declared. The company would be merely a vehicle through which money could be borrowed from members by the issue of redeemable debentures of say £15 each which they could have back on request. Thus the control of the club could not be sold or dispersed without the full approval of the members.

The first plan in 1939 was to build the second nine and raise money by the issue of debentures of £5 each vested in trustees with the object of attracting as many members as possible. These debentures could be drawn gradually with the aim of redeeming the whole issue by the end of the lease. At that time it was thought that £1,500 would be needed. As it turned out no decision to raise money was needed until years later when this latter plan was resurrected and revamped to suit the prevailing circumstances.

FINAL DECISION

The special committees formed must have worked overtime to thrash out all aspects because in March 25th, 1939, they were able to issue a circular to all members. Ideas for improving the existing clubhouse were abandoned in favour of using the farm house and buildings – converting where necessary into changing rooms, professional's shop, caddies' shelter and so on "with a good draw-in and covered car park". As well as the debenture plan an increase in subscription was proposed to supplement the amount.

Entrance fee	£2 .2s. 0d.	Sub. men	£4. 4s. 0d.
Sub. ladies	£3. 3s. 0d.	5 day	£3. 3s. 0d. men
			£2. 2s. 0d. ladies
Radius	£1. 11s. 6d.		

The five day membership was new. The other increases amounted to one guinea full members, half a guinea radius members.

All of which seems very straight forward and contained sound reasoning. Looking at the Dormy House today, one cannot help but feel regret that the plans did not succeed.

PROBLEMS WITH THE FARM TENANT

The first spanner was thrown into the works by Cotterill (these people were always referred to by their surname) the farm tenant. The original terms for quitting the property he had agreed upon with the secretary were verbal and more mature thought persuaded him he had undervalued his assets so he changed his mind. His increased terms were as follows: Two years rent = £140, permission to sell his live and dead stock and manure, permission to remain at the farm till his ewes had lambed, until he had a new house, together with payment of an unspecified sum for the ploughing and seeding which he had already done.

Mr. Booth turned the proposal down flat so Cotterill stated the whole deal was off! Mr. Righton (Evesham estate agent) was appointed as arbitrator but the terms "instead of being lighter than those previously offered, are more arbitrary and irksome", said Mr. Booth. Cotterill won in the end but the club suggested that at least they should be allowed to withhold the rent of £50 payable to Captain Burges until they could take over the premises. The argument had stretched from February until April 1st.

SIGNED AND SEALED AT LAST

At a special committee meeting on July 5th, 1939, a report was discussed covering progress so far, to be made to the general committee. This confirmed that agreement had been reached with the Burgeses to lease the whole farm at a total rental of £175 per annum with option to purchase after the deaths of Captain and Mrs. Burges. The club reported that they had leased surplus land as follows: Arable acres cross the road (that is beyond the present 12th fairway) let to Stewart & Sons, 52 acres – £52 per annum. Grass fields, let to J. Ingles, 22½ acres – £22. 10s per annum. Arable alongside Golf Club, let to J. Webb, 18 acres – £18 0s 0d.

The house was to be let to a suitable tenant who should repair and decorate the interior. He should supply all meals required by members and allow outbuildings to be converted to a clubhouse. On their part the club would grant a lease of seven, fourteen or twenty years. Mr. Pemberton expressed a view "how possibly the best club house in the county can be made out of the existing buildings at comparatively little cost".

But the unsettled international situation persuaded them to shelve all thought of raising extra money for the new nine holes. At a special general meeting on July 13th, 1939, the report was accepted with special thanks to Mr. Pemberton for all the work he had done in preparing plans. Mr. Pemberton replied "stressing his great affection for the old club". There is no evidence to show whether other tenants were sought but the successful application to rent Willersey Hill Farm came from Mr. and Mrs. Guy Pemberton who took an option to lease for 21 years.

Matters connected with the house continued to overshadow all other considerations for the next few years. It seems that sufficient attention was not given to the implications of the lease granted to the Pembertons – it was heavily weighted in their favour and in due course proved to be very disadvantageous to Broadway Golf Club. The club was very dependent on retaining their goodwill and the impression given in the records is that unfortunately the relationship was not sustained due to an accumulation of misunderstandings and inefficiency on both sides. There was some clash of interests – obviously the Pembertons would be looking for a sound, profitable business, whereas the golf club regarded the Dormy as an amenity for members.

Thus at the outbreak of the Second World War we see Broadway Golf Club with an increasing membership, lessees of 170 acres with a farm house, with an option to buy the whole property. Both house and land were profitably let and plans for enlarging the course were all ready. At face value quite a rosy situation. All plans for the course were shelved but the Pembertons took over the house and the various tenants the land – whilst Adolf Hitler was doing his best to take over the whole of Europe.

FOURTH PERIOD 1924–39

1925, club joined Gloucestershire Golf Union.

1925, Founder's Cup in memory of Dr. Standring.

1927, security of tenure improved by adding option of a further seven years.

1929, first motor tractor.

1929, Dr. Mackenzie advises on course.

1931, professional tournament (Gloucester/Somerset Alliance), prize fund £30.

1932, Mr. Cuthbert Rayner Booth appointed honorary secretary.

1933, first water to greens.

1935, Tom Simpson (golf architect) designs 8th hole.

1935, Alexander Cup presented – foursomes knockout.

1938, 21-year lease plus option to purchase all Willersey Hill Farm (signed 1939).

Chapter Five

War Followed by Austerity
1939–50

HIGH HOPES THWARTED

WAR broke out in September. The secretary decided he could not call meetings due to the rationing of petrol and sent out a report to members on what was planned. He used an old-fashioned phrase "The whole of our staff with the exception of Bisgrove has been called to the colours". This meant grass-cutting problems but two boys aged 11 and 12 went after school and Saturday mornings to help. Mr. Booth decided to put sheep on the course again to help keep the grass down and also with the aim of forestalling any order from the War Agricultural Committee to plough up the course for the purpose of growing food. In order to be able to visit the course at least four days a week, Mr. Booth bought himself a bicycle – a pretty strenuous ride up from Mickleton where he lived. But it was Bisgrove who kept the course going. For days on end he was left to work by himself, never seeing a soul. The committee resolved to give him an ex gratia payment of £10 in appreciation.

The one thing Bisgrove could not do was drive a tractor and it was left to the secretary who cut the fairways well into his old age.

FINANCES

At the start of the war in spite of a falling off of green fees and a reduction in subscriptions, the balance was over £20 up on the previous year. Agreement reached with Mr. Pemberton meant that light, water and drainage should be supplied to the house, the cost of the work to be met out of capital. But the rents received would be £22 10s in excess of what was needed to meet commitments to Captain Burges. The improvements to the house were expected to cost around £250 – more than had been anticipated but the war was pushing up prices. In April, 1940 the finances were in a fair position. Even after £390 had been paid out in non-recurring expenses the investment was still intact at £150 and the deposit account of entrance fees amounted to £61.

For their part Mr. and Mrs. Pemberton handed over to the club "the side entrance with Games Room, lavatory etc. as well as the main sitting room in front with the right to partake of all meals in the Dining Room". This would seem to have been an ideal arrangement but time proved it was fraught with snags. Now that Bisgrove was so occupied with the course he was not always available to collect green fees so arrangements were made for money to be collected at the house. The problem was that the amount of money available did not marry up with what Bisgrove estimated there should be or by comparison with the "book". This inefficient collecting method was serious as the club depended on green fees for income. It was eventually agreed that tickets from a book with accompanying counterfoil would provide a check and Mr. Pemberton was asked to meet Bisgrove at a fixed time each week to settle accounts. By 1941 it was stated that the arrangements were working satisfactorily but this proved only temporary, deteriorating when new tenants became involved. There were other niggling matters in the early years of the war – who should control the pumping of the water? Mr. Pemberton demanded he should have sole control, which on reflection Mr. Booth was happy to grant as it relieved him and the club of responsibility. It was alleged that the wind pump had been broken by Mr. Pemberton and the club's tank was having to be filled by overflow from the Dormy House. Continuing the list of petty disagreements and misunderstandings, Mr. Pemberton was anxious about storing Mr. Stewart's wheat in the Dutch barn which the club had rented to him for a very small sum. Mr. Stewart was chivied to move it as Mr. Pemberton was anxious about incendiary bombs!

A glance at the balance sheet for 1940 shows that the repairs and improvements carried out at the Dormy House was easily the largest item of expenditure:

Water supply	£125 7s 5d
Electricity	40 0s 0d
Drainage	87 0s 0d
Plumbing	7 16s 1d
Walling	3 0s 1d
Law costs	26 6s 7d

But the committee were still optimistic and hoped that at the end of hostilities they would carry on where they left off before the start of the war. As the bank balance was increasing due to the income from the land, they were happy with the additional comfort which the Dormy House provided as a clubhouse, and it seems that they allowed the "hut" to run down, merely using it as somewhere to change shoes and eventually store machinery.

There was no reason why any doubts should be felt in spite of the few problems. After all, Mr. Pemberton had been a friend of the club since its inception in 1895. By September 26th, 1943 Captain Burges had died. The position of the club was briefly discussed at an informal meeting, reference being made to the arrangements for purchase. It was pointed out that any improvements made by the club would be taken into account when the purchase price was fixed. Surely anyone buying Farncombe after the death of Mrs. Burges "would welcome the land at the back being used as a golf club, besides the amenity caused by such use". The members present at the meeting felt that the comfort of the Dormy House cum clubhouse must be further enhanced to attract new members but "The question of financing any such improvement was barely discussed".

Dr. Alexander's putting style

Dr. Alexander and son Gordon

FURTHER DEVELOPMENT

No meeting was then held until March 7th, 1945 when the chicken of the 21 year lease granted to Mr. and Mrs. Pemberton came home to roost. By now Mrs. Burges had also died. A new company had taken over Farncombe calling itself the Farncombe Estate Company. Both Mr. and Mrs. Pemberton were involved. The chief investor was a Mr. Titchmarsh, a businessman from Childswickham, who gave a report to the meeting on the new company and requested that the lease granted to Mrs. Pemberton on the Dormy House be assigned to the new company. It was proposed to capitalise Mrs. Pemberton's goodwill and furniture at the Dormy to cover her financial obligation in the company and she would then become salaried manageress of the Farncombe House Country Club, with complete control of both this and the Dormy House.

Mrs. Pemberton was to move to Farncombe and put in a manager at the Dormy House but if she wanted to return no obstacle had to be put in her way by the golf club. She was to be responsible for catering and accommodation at both places, Farncombe to be the more expensive.

Mr. Titchmarsh commented that the golf club was an asset for the company who would possibly be willing to put forward cash when the time came to embark on the 18 hole course!

One can speculate what might have happened if this company had been allowed to play any financial part in the improvement of the golf course. After dropping the bombshell, Messrs. Titchmarsh and Pemberton withdrew from the meeting. Left to themselves the committee members were obviously disconcerted. They had been placed in a position over which they had no control and could find no legal way to deny Mrs. Pemberton's right to transfer the lease. Having decided that a friendly agreement was the best solution, wishing to avoid disappointed and disgruntled people running the Dormy House, the club inserted a proviso that if Mrs. Pemberton ever withdrew, then the club would cancel the assignment of the lease to the company. But the relevant reports show how the balance was weighing heavily in favour of Mrs. Pemberton and against the golf club. Suggestions from Mr. Booth that as the club would be a substantial asset to the company they should pay extra rent or build the club a new clubhouse were dismissed summarily by Mr. Titchmarsh but he suggested again that "arrangements to merge the two interests should be given consideration" – without doubt a shrewd businessman.

Mr. H. O. Roberts

The club made a fortuitous choice when they instructed Mr. H. O. Roberts (solicitor) to act on their behalf. "Bonzo" as he eventually was known, with his wife Madge, were to become among the leaders of the club out of the post-war doldrums. It was Mr. Roberts whose advice eventually set the club on a successful financial path. He was not a member of the club at this time, not yet being a Broadway resident, but due to his work in establishing the new company, he was elected an honorary member of the company.

The Continuing Saga

Immediately after the meeting with Farncombe representatives, a valuation was put in hand of the improvements carried out by Mrs. Pemberton at the Dormy House. These amounted to £776 0s 0d. New managers were found, a Mr. and Mrs. Gilbertson. As these people were total strangers to the club, arrangements for collecting green fees and selling drinks had to be tightened up – it had to be made perfectly clear to the new managers what was expected of them – *but* they were employed by and therefore under the control of Mrs. Pemberton and the Farncombe Company to whom her lease was assigned. At a meeting in May 1945, it was candidly agreed by Messrs. Titchmarsh and Saunders (the company solicitor) "that the agreement was completely one-sided, giving Mrs. Pemberton rights which were never understood by the club" (namely *full* control of the Dormy House). However in writing his report Mr. Booth stresses that the matter was discussed in an atmosphere of great friendliness. The weakness of the minutes is that they were quite subjective.

The matter was settled by June 9th, 1945.

OPTION TO PURCHASE, 1945

Now both Captain and Mrs. Burges were dead, it was possible to put the plan to purchase the whole of Willersey Hill Farm into operation. A valuation was prepared by Mr. Righton, and a purchase price of £4,650 was suggested and eventually agreed upon. Thought had once more to be given to raising the money and a circular to all members was sent out June 28th, 1945.

It is proposed to raise the necessary money by the issue of Debentures either vested in Trustees or in a private company, such debentures to be in denominations of £10 and carrying 4% interest. Each year a certain number to be drawn for, and paid off at an agreed extra price.

In order to issue debentures a new company had to be formed. This was to be a private limited liability company and it was suggested that all fully paid up members of October 1st, 1945, should be allotted one share value 10/- and anyone joining later should pay 10/- extra to their entrance fee. Thus the company would be limited by guarantee (10/- each member) which everyone would forfeit if problems arose, and this situation remains basically the same today, although the sum involved now seems very trifling.

The members were asked for promises of £10 to reach a maximum of £6,000. Captain Butler, the vendor of the property had promised to leave a sum of £1,000 on debenture. It was not until May 1946 that articles of association were completed by Mr. Roberts. Lloyds Bank was to be asked to act as trustees. On formation of the new Broadway Golf Club Limited, the old Broadway Golf Club would be dissolved and the general committee elected at the AGM would become the board of directors.

At a meeting on September 4th, 1946, it was decided that for the moment debenture issue should not exceed the purchase price of £4,650 and that Captain Butler's offer of £1,000 should not be taken up. They had actual subscriptions and promises exceeding the amount needed for purchase, but over 50 per cent of a much reduced membership had shown no interest and it was felt that a wider spread of debentures would be better for club and members alike. By December 1946 debentures up to £4,000 had finally been subscribed. The new Broadway Golf Club Ltd was to take over all the assets and liabilities of the old Broadway Golf Club. The Registrar General would now require a properly audited balance sheet so a qualified person had to be appointed as assistant secretary to deal with company matters on a paid basis. Mr. Ogden of Lloyds Bank, Evesham, was employed at an inclusive fee of £30. 10s.

So it seemed all was well. The road ahead for Broadway Golf Club Limited looked smooth but in fact it proved to be quite bumpy.

MORE DIFFICULTIES WITH THE HOUSE

The purchasing and selling of drinks at the Dormy continued to be a problem. As the hon. sec. was responsible for the licence, it was undesirable that Mr. Titchmarsh should be allowed to interfere in the supply. Mr. Gilbertson was instructed to lock the cellar! A veteran member says that there were problems over some members' late night drinking and as the hon. sec. was a local JP it is not difficult to imagine a possible scenario. By November 1945, the Gilbertsons were leaving the Dormy House and their replacement was the Hutchinsons. Once more profit on drinks was unsatis- factory – the safety of storage again open to question. In 1946 Farncombe Estates complained that their share of the profits from the bar made the present arrangements completely uneconomical – they were told by the club that the main object of the bar was to be an amenity rather than make a large profit. This was no doubt the antithesis of Farncombe's policy. Finally figures were extracted showing a debt to the club by Farncombe Estates of £84 19s 4d in July 1947. Mr. Pemberton was "very hurt" at receiv- ing no friendly warning of an impending letter from the club solicitors. There is no record that Farncombe ever paid.

Soon the Farncombe Estates decided to cease offering full board at the Dormy House. It was obviously not succeeding as a profit-making concern. The club was further disquieted by news that the RDC were taking an inter- est with a view to requisitioning it when vacant.

This precipitated action. Farncombe Estates gave five weeks' notice to quit, thus nullifying the tenancy agreement, leaving the golf club free to take over the running of the Dormy House. They advertised for new managers "to live rent free in return for specified services to golf club". The bar was officially moved to the old club hut on the course.

Meanwhile Mrs. Pemberton made an inventory of her fixtures and fittings for which she hoped to receive suitable recompense but most of her furniture was removed. The golf club directors furnished the rooms they were to use "with any suitable furniture as gifts or at reasonable cost they could acquire". The Johnsons, who had taken over, were lent sufficient things to enable the Dormy House to re-open – hardly a businesslike situation.

PRE-WAR HOPES DASHED – FALLING MEMBERSHIP – FINANCIAL CRISIS

June 1947 saw the first inkling of expenditure exceeding money in hand. Mr. Ogden pointed out that cheques had been prepared for signature. When added to accounts for machinery repairs which had yet to come in, the company's account must inevitably go into debit before the financial year end. Extended overdraft facilities were requested and an attempt was to be made to incur only essential expenditure. Although assets would provide ample security the bank manager, Mr. Eaton, felt that the request would not be looked on with favour by Lloyds Bank. The directors of the club considered the issue of more debentures to cover the deficit and anticipated future losses but were advised this would be unwise as it would be to cover trading losses not purchase of assets and unfair to existing debenture holders. This is the situation which is recorded but rumour adds that some members were asking for their debentures to be realised. The coup de grace was delivered when Mr. Eaton recommended "that the Directors should seriously consider the advisability of realising all assets not required for the actual running of the nine hole course and thus put Broadway Golf Club Limited into a firm financial position".

In one sense this was understandable as the directors of the club were neither hoteliers nor property developers but the value of the assets was quite considerable. The post-war boom in golf was still a few years away and who then, could have foreseen it?

Mr. Rayner Booth was upset as the selling of the Dormy House would curtail any club extension and the Johnsons, the managers put in by the club, would lose home and job in one blow. It was stated at this time that "the possibility of the Company being able to extend the course to an eighteen hole one was remote".

The idea was put forward that when debentures were paid off the balance could be used to build a new clubhouse with accommodation for a steward but worries were expressed that if they hung on to part of the acreage "land values might well fall". By August 1948 a resolution was passed at an EGM that the house and spare land should be sold. The chairman explained the reason "rent etc. covered mortgage interest but the subscriptions, green fees etc. did not bring in sufficient income to cover the running of the golf course as well as the expense of owning the Dormy House, so that the club was faced with the prospect of an annual deficit unless income were increased or expenses decreased". We all owe a debt of gratitude to some unknown member of the committee who suggested a rider to the resolution, namely that *all* the land should not be sold unless absolutely necessary.

The Dormy House in the 1950s

The sum of £7,000 was hoped for from the sale of the Dormy House but in the end £5,500 was accepted from a Miss Hanson, in February 1949. The club was to rent one room as their Club Room. Possession of a few outbuildings and the fold yard was retained. The matter of the settlement in cash to Mr. Pemberton for his improvements was dealt with by Mr. Roberts who paid over £1,000 from his own account as a loan free of interest – a very generous gesture.

The repayment of cash to the debenture holders was considered but delayed for the time being. But at a meeting May 1st, 1949, the view was expressed that there should be no further delay in selling land surplus to what would be required for any future extension to the course; it was to be offered to the tenants at a proposed price of £1,500. Thus the total received from all sales would be £7,000, out of which the debentures amounting to £4,300 plus interest, had to be repaid as well as the debt of £1,000 to Mr. Roberts. On November 22nd Mr. Ogden announced that the club had made a profit of £11 11s 6d and cash in solicitor's hands amounted to £1,651 18s 5d. So ten years of financial ebb and flow came to an end.

One cause of the difficulties in which the club found itself was the fact that although hostilities finished in 1945, Britain remained in the grip of austerity until the mid 1950s. It was originally thought that a doubling of membership was necessary to warrant extension of the course; the committee felt this could be achieved. This optimism was misplaced for the time being as the opposite happened. In 1949 the hon. sec. reported membership of 164 (men 120, ladies 44), compared with 257 in 1938. "If I get a new member, another drops out", he bemoaned. As well as the lack of membership he was constantly complaining of apathy among existing members, just as before the war. It was still difficult to fill the competitions and the interest in the monthly medal was virtually nil. A story about this is told by Harold Haydon, now the second longest serving member of the golf club. He says he was very keen to win a monthly medal and thought his chance had come when only two people entered, Ian Tilbrook and himself – he still came second and has never yet managed to achieve his ambition!

Thus the club embarked upon the next decade with a small amount of capital. They had gained the advantage of being able to purchase the land they used plus the extra to extend to 18 holes. Surplus to immediate needs were one or two out buildings at the Dormy House and the field below the 6th. Lack of income had forced them to part with what could have been a very valuable asset, namely the Dormy House. Even today people voice the opinion that this was a mistake, but at the time it was sell or risk bankruptcy – unless members were prepared to pay higher subscriptions, but this was never a popular option.

FIFTH PERIOD, 1939–50

1943, death of Captain Burges.

1945, purchase of Willersey Hill Farm for £4,650.

1946, formation of Broadway Golf Club Limited.

1947, end of lease to Fancombe Estates Ltd for Dormy House.

1948, Mr. Eaton (manager, Lloyds Bank, Broadway) advises sale of surplus assets.

1948, EGM Aug. 2nd resolution to sell Dormy House with or without 90/100 acres of land passed unanimously.

1949, Dormy House Hotel sold to Miss Hanson for £5,500.

1949, death of Dr. Alexander.

1949, sale of 52 acres of land from present 12th hole to picnic area, price £1,500.

Secretary's Notes

This last year has been an eventful one in the Club's History, as many important things have been carried out.

After much negotiation, the sale of the Dormy House to Miss Hanson was completed. The price, while not being quite as good as we had hoped for, was nevertheless a satisfactory one.

By means of this sale we were able to :—

Redeem the whole Debenture Issue.

Pay Mr. Pemberton his "Improvements" agreed upon and carried-out by him during his tenancy.

In addition, the surplus land, lying between the Road and Fish Hill has been sold to the tenants Stewart & Sons.

The sum total of these dealings has provided the Club with a substantial balance, which can be drawn upon for necessary improvements to Club House etc.

Your Secretary still anticipates that he will be able, as in the past, to pay the running expenses of the Club out of subscriptions, green fees and rents.

Members are reminded that the Club still possess some 120 acres sufficient to carry-out the extension of the Course to 18 holes, if and when it is thought advisable.

Secretary Rayner Booth keeps members up to date, 1949

Chapter Six

A Dream Finally Fulfilled
1950–62

Approach to Expansion

ALTHOUGH the early 1950s continued to be a struggle, this next period was probably the most important in the whole history of Broadway Golf Club in that it eventually saw the extension from 9 to 18 holes. The president who held office for the whole of the 1950s until the new 9 holes were completed was Mr. Charles Gardiner. After the resignation of Dr. Alexander in 1946, before his death in 1949, the ubiquitous Mr. Rayner Booth had taken over the presidency in 1947 (along with his honorary secretaryship and membership of house, greens and handicap committees). The steadying influence of Mr. Gardiner was said to be of great value.

Dogged by Lack of Cash

The course itself had taken a back seat during the turmoil years of the war and then the buying and selling of land became the prime interest. Now the club was again faced with lack of funds due to falling membership. In 1951 an increase in new members was cancelled out by resignations – total membership 160, of whom 19 were new but 21 resigned. The bad weather of the 1951 season meant green fees were down by £44 as well as subscriptions by £38. 1952 was no better, membership being reduced once more to 136. Various methods of raising money were discussed. Should subscriptions be raised to £6 6 0d? An error on the part of Mr. Booth meant that members were not informed and complaints led to other means being considered. Should a small fee be paid every time a member played? Regular playing members were invited to pay £1 1s 0d over and above the subscription. This notion sank without trace, only three donations were received, a total of £2 7s 6d. The treasurer thought that strong efforts should be made to increase the club's income. The £1,000 worth of defence bonds were sold, an amount used to pay for painting the clubhouse and £800 re-invested in 3 ½ per cent bonds. But still income fell. 1953 income was down £26, green fees down £15. Expenses had to be cut and it was in this atmosphere that Mr. Rayner Booth began to feel his years and the greenkeeper resigned. This left Bisgrove as the only member of staff, who before the war had three helpers on the course.

BISGROVE – AN ENIGMA?

To some a hard working servant of the club, to others a slacker who did not always do his best. Which?

In July 1952 a rather sad little homily appears in the minutes from Mr. Rayner Booth "I am beginning to feel my age and I don't like cold winds and wet weather, with the result that sometimes the tractor could have gone out but I did not feel up to it. This is no passing phase but will increase as time goes on and members must really think what they are going to do. With a balance of £163 there is not enough in the kitty to employ outside labour even if we could get it." As during the war when he kept the course going, the answer was Bisgrove – Ernest Foulkes left in 1952, the hon. sec. was becoming feeble, Bisgrove became professional and greenkeeper. The snag was he could not drive a tractor and here a member, Mr. Dalrymple, filled the gap. This dual role, as well as any teaching must have been onerous. Was too much expected of him, especially when the secretary went on holiday in 1954? An EGM was called on 27th July 1954, to discuss the condition of the course and the greens in particular, many complaints having been made. The secretary was indignant and proceeded to support Bisgrove to the hilt stating that he himself had 30 years and Bisgrove 34 years experience of green-keeping whilst "you the signatories (i.e. of the EGM) have not had five minutes let alone years at the job". Prominent members of the club voiced their criticisms – P. O. Heatherley said he had lost all confidence in Bisgrove, G. E. Knight commented the course had gone from bad to worse, greens, fairways and tees were deplorable. One, K. Grove had "an unfortunate experience with soot". The aim of the soot was to prevent fusarian patch which it did because it burnt off all the grass. Someone said "Broadway greens are infinitely the worst in the area".

And so on … Mr. Clifton, a future captain, commented "the condition of the course after the resolution was written, improved out of all knowledge". Much can be read into this comment. The secretary tendered his resignation (again!) but reconsidered after a vote of full confidence. Cryptically in his final remarks, the president pointed out that Bisgrove had a different sense of humour to many people and what was a joke to him might appear to be rudeness to others.

Trying to smooth his ruffled feathers, a life membership for Mr. Rayner Booth was considered. Indeed after over 30 years of unstinting effort for Broadway Golf Club he deserved some recompense, overlooking the fact that he could be high-handed and difficult, offending many people. The honorary life membership was finally awarded in April 1956. An oak seat was bought in his honour (cost £20) and suitably inscribed and Mr. Dalrymple took over the job of hon. sec. As for Bisgrove he continued as before, professional/greenkeeper, cum clubhouse cleaner, plus efforts on his own behalf in poultry-keeping in a spare hut and vegetable growing on a patch of land down near the 2nd tee as well as growing his own tobacco in the room which later became the ladies' lounge, according to "Recollections" by Madge Roberts.

Presentation of oak seat in honour of Mr. Rayner Booth – 3rd from right – 1956 (inscribed in error Raynor Booth)

THE COURSE AND GOLF

Only work of a minor nature was undertaken in the early 1950s, the continued falling membership, lack of money, with only one paid member of staff restricting progress.

In 1951, par was fixed at 70 with SSS 69. All handicaps therefore needed revision. This was made more difficult because some members never returned cards for handicap review – one won the Lloyd Cup playing off 12 when everyone knew he should have been less. The committee cut him to 10 – his name can remain lost in the minutes!

Ladies were invited to play in the monthly medal and special terms were introduced for teenagers, 1/- a day, 21/- per annum. An attempt was made to get a mutual arrangement with Evesham Golf Club for full members to play either course for £1 1s 0d added to their sub. Evesham declined.

A small amount of machinery was bought – 1951, a new Fergusson paraffin tractor, 1953, a 20" Atco mower for the greens and new lighter aluminium flagpoles. The secretary was in hot water with the committee on account of his buying machinery and tools himself, lending them to the club and then asking for payment. 1953 saw the introduction of the County Card – for a fee of 10/- members were allowed to play free on county courses.

An interesting comment appears in the minutes regarding the bunker on the left of the 9th green – it was decided to make this into a sand bunker to give members practice at playing out of sand when they visited other courses. Did this mean that none of the Broadway bunkers contained sand at this time?

The course in the 1950s

5th green

7th green

MEMBERSHIP

In 1956 membership at Broadway was down again – 122 reduced to 117. The treasurer pointed out that the club's surplus related to capital arising out of judicious sales of property, not revenue. He thought attempts should be made to increase the balance in hand, any unforseen expense would have to be met out of capital. It was suggested that an increase in subscription should be considered; Broadway's subscription was below other local clubs and Evesham was considering putting theirs up to £6 6s 0d. Suggested rises were:

Men from	£5 5s 0d	to	£6 6s 0d
Ladies	£3 3s 0d		£3 10s 0d
Green fees	2s 6d		3s 6d
Saturday, Sunday holidays	5s 0d		6s 0d

These were approved in April, 1956.

In 1951 the Dormy House had been sold again by Miss Hanson to Misses Mackay and Holt. At the same time the club accepted an offer of £50 from these ladies for the fold yard and one or two outbuildings which still belonged to them. The club still owned further buildings by the Dormy House and a way of raising money was to sell these. There was a suggestion that they could be converted into a house and then sold, but this was taken no further.

Generally there had been an upsurge in golf club membership in the mid 1950s which had not yet found Broadway. Probably they were again suffering from the isolated position, making transport of some nature a necessity.

Suddenly the turn around came. In August, 1957 green fees were up and membership fees doubled. Broadway was starting to catch up.

Discussion took place whether medal competitions should start from two tees to avoid congestion – something of a change from when Mr. Rayner Booth could hardly get enough players to make it worth starting at all. The question was raised of whether membership should be limited or the course enlarged? It was to be another two years before action was taken.

TO WATER OR NOT TO WATER

The old watering system had been abandoned years ago on advice from the Research Station at Bingley, because it was felt that watering had a bad effect on the natural grasses which formed the basis of Broadway greens. 1956 had been very dry then in 1957, when traffic on the course began to increase, it was decided to inspect the old system. By August all pipes had been located and plotted on a map and by the end of the year were being repaired. Tanks were purchased to be put on the highest point of the course, which is on the left of the present 17th by the fir tree which catches so many bad drives. Mr. Heatherley was to have full control of the greens.

Staff

A little extra affluence meant thoughts of additional labour. Bisgrove's duties were to be defined more clearly – he was relieved of his clubhouse cleaning and greenkeeping and told he should now concentrate on lessons and selling equipment. A new man, Howley, was employed for part of the year. He was to be paid £7 14s 0d per week and Bisgrove reduced to £5 0s 0d per week plus 10 per cent of green fees. This made a big improvement on the course but to keep Howley permanently would need £400 a year. As usual the committee wanted to avoid raising fees and it was suggested that Bisgrove accept a permanent £5 0s 0d and augment it himself. It seems quite astonishing. As well as this Howley asked for and was granted a loan to buy a motor cycle.

Ladies

It was during the 1950s that a group of enthusiastic lady golfers became members, the first since the days of Mrs. and Miss Alexander. The ladies' room had never been very comfortable and was severely criticised in 1955 by Mrs. Pritchard and Mrs. Roberts. They were allowed £40 for improvements. The items the ladies considered bare necessities were a door mat, a large mirror with a cupboard underneath, notice board, soap and nail-brush, lockers, curtains, teapot, kettle, crockery. Mrs. Roberts was to purchase towels and arrange laundering. As there were only seven names on the ladies' list in 1956 this seems quite generous. The ladies wished to apply for re-admission to the LGU but only four had handicaps, a minimum of six was required – it was going to be an uphill battle.

The Gardiner "Cup" 1957. From left: S. Pritchard, C.H. Gardiner, A. Ellis, unknown, N. Gorin, P. Thornhill, J. Hoskins, B. Stanley, M. Roberts, unknown, K. Stockdale, unknown

The president offered a prize for a ladies' competition, this is still played for, namely the Gardiner Cup. The first winner in 1957 was Miss Joan Hoskins. At the first presentation the "cup" was a golf club, as can be seen in the photograph.

The first joint captain and secretary of the rejuvenated section was Miss Joan Hoskins whilst Mrs. Madge Roberts was to be clubhouse supervisor, a job which she did thoroughly. She often did cleaning of both ladies' room and lounge and was happy wielding a paint brush when necessary. The ladies' section began raising money to provide furniture for the general lounge, to supplement £100 which had been allowed for the purpose. It was stipulated that this had to include 12 chairs and tables for meetings. The ladies' section remained a tight knit, keen group of golfers, several of whom, although long gone, are still well known today on account of trophies named in their honour, for example the Kathleen Stockdale and Barbara Stanley Cups. Gradually more trophies were introduced as membership increased. The Madge Roberts three club competition was started in 1958. 1960 saw the introduction of the Silver Salver. There were seven entries, and a rule stipulated that the first eight qualify! The Winifred Stevens trophy for medal winners (re-admission to the LGU had been granted) was first played for in 1962. There were seven players. The Ladies Greensome was started in 1959 with six couples entering. By 1972 entry had increased to 20 couples. There were 32 entrants in the first Ladies Open in 1969. It is interesting to note that the first "Bring and Win" (a nine-hole competition, each player to bring a small prize) followed by the AGM was introduced in 1957. This competition has been repeated annually until 1995 when, to please one or two low handicap ladies, an 18-hole medal round was played. At the subsequent meeting by a strong vote in favour, the "Bring and Win" was reinstated.

JENNY – A NAME SYNONYMOUS WITH BROADWAY LADIES

The late 1950s saw the arrival of Miss Jennifer Foxon at Broadway Golf Club. More than 35 years on, Jenny still plays off single figures and has been lady champion more times than anyone. Her arrival was described by Mrs. Madge Roberts.

The next lady to put in an appearance was Miss Jennifer Foxon. I shall always remember the day when just starting out in a 3 ball, one of the others mentioned there was a lady in the clubhouse. Should we offer her a game? We of course agreed and out walked Jennifer. I enquired what her handicap was and she said she didn't have one. I was a "big-headed" 27 then so I promptly offered her shots off 36. Was my face red when her drive on the 2nd reached the green! Jennifer started to put in her cards and was soon down to single figures.

This was the start of a very successful golfing career. Her achievements over

BROADWAY GOLF CLUB – LADY CAPTAINS
ON THE OCCASION OF THE 80th BIRTHDAY OF

MARGARET ROBERTS
10th NOVEMBER 1983

JOAN WALKER   WIN THORPE   JENNYFOXON   ANN SHORT
GWEN KNIGHT   JOAN HOSKINS   ELEANOR FEAVER
MARGARET CAUDWELL   FIL COOKE   DAPHNE TILBROOK   KATH JENNINGS
MARY CAVE   ANN BOOTH   STELLA STACEY   PAM CHAPMAN
MARGARET ROBERTS

Mrs. M. Roberts 80th birthday

the years are numerous. Jennifer eventually took over the running of the bar at the club and on her retirement in 1995 became the vice captain of Gloucestershire Ladies.

The 1950s definitely saw the arrival of the ladies section at Broadway Golf Club and it is flourishing more than ever today.

THE CLUBHOUSE

During the Dormy House days the clubhouse had been allowed to deteriorate and had to be improved. In 1950 there was no electricity. There were Calor gas stoves but no lights. Water was available but an interesting point appears in a meeting in 1951. There was a reading of 57,000 gallons on the meter instead of 570 gallons. The hon. sec. said he guessed what was happening "and it was so". It is quite infuriating that he says no more.

In 1952 gas light was installed in the clubhouse at a cost of £6 0s 0d but members kept breaking the mantles. In 1955 the old chestnut of a house being built for a steward and his wife was once more raised because taking meals at the Dormy was unsatisfactory. A new shop was needed for Bisgrove as well as improved light and heat; electricity was still not connected. The secretary felt vehemently this was unnecessary capital expenditure and once more reminded members how much money he saved them – and they were actually considering squandering money on electricity! When he was away ill in April 1956, lighting was installed as well as two water heaters and four Belling heaters. The following year electric fires were placed in the changing rooms and finally the telephone, but by this time Mr. Booth had retired.

SURPLUS LAND – CHANGE AT THE DORMY HOUSE

The club solicitor, Mr. Roberts, the value of whose expertise and business acumen cannot be exaggerated, was asked to obtain details of rents and tenancy of all land adjoining the course. There were no written agreements and the club wanted to raise rents, sell the surplus; in other words formalise the situation. The field below the 6th was tenanted by Mr. Ingles who offered to buy it for £100 but a Mr. Riley raised this to £140. The field above the 1st rented by Mr. Everett, Captain Hannay's agent, had a rent rise from £20 to £35, whilst the two fields behind the Dormy House, now occupied by Mr. Ingles, were to cost £45 instead of £22 10s. He undertook to keep these fields in permanent pasture until needed by the golf club. This was to prove very useful when members finally decided to build the new nine holes themselves; they were simply able to mow the fields. The sale of the buildings and fold yard affected Mr. Ingles' tenancy so in lieu he was offered the sheds now occupied by Bisgrove's poultry. By October 1956, the sales were completed and brought in £190. The raised rents meant double previous receipts.

Another Legal Complication with Mr. Pemberton

An interesting legal situation arose in 1955 when a letter was received from Guy Pemberton to the secretary.

On the bill of sale from Alan Butler to the golf club of November 5th, 1946, it is laid down that he and his family, friends and relations staying with him at Farncombe, play golf free gratis plus any guest of Alan Butler or "owner for the time being of Farncombe". Guy Pemberton having just bought Farncombe said this now applied to his family and son's friends "so will you please see that he is entered on the club lists as a full member". The committee felt this issue could become very important so they instructed Mr. Roberts to offer Mr. Pemberton's son David life membership, providing the whole of the clause in the conveyance was deleted. If this had been allowed and Farncombe continued as an hotel, who knows how many people would feel entitled to play for nothing?

The New Nine Holes, EGM 1958

The nettle had at last to be grasped. It was becoming clear that if Broadway was to keep up with the general trend of an increasing number of people wishing to play golf then the proposed extension to eighteen holes must be seriously considered. The club membership had increased to 163. Remarkably, 43 of these were ladies. As Mr. Ian Tilbrook said when opening the proceedings, "This is a momentous meeting". The aim of the evening was to discuss and decide whether or not to increase to eighteen holes. The land was available and the tenants had always understood that it would have to be relinquished one day for use of the club, fields having been kept down to grass for the purpose.

Mr. Tilbrook pointed out the three alternatives avilable. The committee had formulated a plan for 18 holes, using one field at present rented by Captain Hannay through his agent; a sub committee had thought out a 15 hole course; then there was the Braid plan from 1938, 18 holes using the three fields right down to the clubhouse. Members voiced worries about the cost of laying out nine more holes. A common fear was that the extension might spoil the pleasant nine they already had. A pertinent comment was made: "If we go for the eighteen hole course, based on increased membership on the financial side, there will be no increase in membership until we have got the eighteen hole course." In other words money would have to be found in the immediate event. Understandably, the 15 holes plan found no

89

favour and the final option was leave the course at nine or the Braid plan – no real choice! This would mean only slight alteration to the existing nine: the 1st and 2nd had to be slipped down the hill in order to accommodate the new 17th and 18th. The short wall which we now see alongside the 17th green used to stretch all the way up to the road, separating what was the old 1st hole from the grass fields which were to be taken over by the new "top nine". This had to be removed but on the whole the members got their wish. The original course was left alone.

Annual Dinner Dance at the Lygon Arms, Broadway 1955. Trophy winners: K. Grove, Dr. Juckes (Founders Cup), J. Gorin (Lloyd Cup), B.A. Strong and H.A. Young (Alexander Foursomes)

It was realised at this meeting in 1958 that the clubhouse facilities would be totally inadequate for the increased membership and visitors they hoped to encourage. But like Scarlet O'Hara it was decided to postpone thinking about this until tomorrow. There was some vague mention of use of the buildings still owned attached to the Dormy House (the section by the present 11th green) and improvements to the clubhouse. It must be remembered that this so called clubhouse, although altered and enlarged with new wooden sheds, still included the one opened in 1912 and commemorated by the match between Arthur Balfour, Hugo Charteris, Spenser Flower and Herbert Asquith. It was eventually all removed but part of it still stands on Jack Gorin's old nursery, Badsey Road, Evesham. At the end of the meeting the chairman, Mr. Charles Gardiner, stated "that unanimity had been reached which he hasn't seen for 20 years".

Annual Dinner Dance at the Lygon Arms, Broadway 1960. Standing l to r: G. Chandler, J. Gorin,
L.G. Dobson, Dr. Mansell, G. Hart, L. Reynolds, P.M. Linder, Dr. Juckes, G. Knight. Sitting l to r:
M. Roberts, K. Jennings, C. Gardiner, H.O. Roberts

Annual Dinner Dance at the Lygon Arms, Broadway 1962. Standing l to r: Graham Horton, Les
Yardley, 'Nig' Gorin, Jack Gorin, Phil Cooke, George Chandler, George Knight, Harry Strong, 'Bonzo'
Roberts.
*   Sitting l to r: Cheryl Price, Kathleen Stockdale, Eileen Booth, Madge Roberts, Kathleen Gorin,*
Peggy Ingles, Pam Vivien

The committee obtained a full written report from the C. K. Cotton partnership, golf architects of Reading. The outstanding item of this report was the estimated cost of the extension to the course based on the Braid plan amounting to £3,930. This was without water being laid on to the greens. The architects expressed the opinion that 18 holes would require three green staff in summer and two in winter as well as two gang mowers and two tractors.

There was no point in discussion. The club simply could not afford it. The committee put in hand experimental work in the field behind the clubhouse, marking out provisional greens and mowing to form fairways. Members were encouraged to try these holes. The results must have been encouraging because by the AGM in January 1960, everyone agreed that the new nine should be built by direct labour – mainly members.

There is no written record of how the job was tackled but many of the people involved are still members and information is readily found. Thanks are due to Mr. P. O. Heatherley (the man who way back in 1934 had been so at odds with Mr. Booth) for heavy involvement in preparing the new greens. Mr. Graham Haydon, a local farmer, was always at hand with heavy equipment. In fact the same tractor and trailer that were used in building the new holes were brought to the course to be on show during the Centennial Fun Night, June 16th, 1995. Jack Gorin who became captain in 1962 tells of dashing up to the course after spending all day in his

Outside Frank Bisgrove's shop the day the new 9 holes opened, April 21st 1962

92

glasshouses when work was in progress on the 14th. He was just in time to prevent the big thorn bush on the right of the fairway from being totally uprooted (in fact it still grows at an angle). Whilst this bush is too far from the tee to cause trouble to most ladies, it has been roundly cursed by gentleman players probably thousands of times over the past 35 years. Thanks to Mr. Gorin for his shrewd anticipation. The same gentleman also preserved the club's ancient monument from total destruction when the 15th green was being made. This monument is an Iron Age fort and Long Barrow – clearly discernible from the contours of the ground between the 14th and 15th holes. The law does not allow the ground to be disturbed even to plant a tree without permission so it was as well that like the Seventh Cavalry, Jack arrived in the nick of time. The Ministry of the Environment require the preservation order to be read aloud at every AGM of the club.

There are many anecdotes which could be told of the building of the new nine. Like the day when Graham Haydon (the farmer with the tractor) had arranged to play his brother Harold, at 8–30am. He went up to the course very early and dug out the bunker on the 10th – his brother was unaware of this till his ball went in it! There is the story of "Sutton's Folly" – the bunker behind the 14th. The green was so sloping that balls constantly rolled down as far as the wall. The bunker was meant to catch them. Stories like this could fill several pages. In fact one wonders how much like the original Braid Plan the new nine holes turned out to be.

The project was completed at the start of 1962 and opened on April 21st. At the AGM in January the president, Mr. Gardiner commented "the past year had been one of remarkable achievement and after the project had been mooted 24 years ago the club had at last put itself in a position where they could start the season with 18 holes". The economical manner in which it had been done was noteworthy. Contractors were charging up to £1,500 per hole; Broadway laid out an additional nine holes from existing financial resources although one long-standing member comments that it was quite rough compared with what we have now. Apparently when buttercups were in full bloom players would come in wearing "yellow shoes". But the achievement of an 18 hole course at so little cost is very impressive.

Administration

Thought was given to the articles of association. These were amended and re-ordered until they were pretty much in the form we know them today, clearly stating who should be the officers and directors of the club, how long they should serve, when they could be re-elected. Jack Gorin was the first vice captain to be appointed, in 1961, the following year becoming

On the 10th tee about to play the extended course April 21st 1962, l to r: C. Gardiner, F. Bisgrove,
W.D. Dalrymple, C. Rayner Booth, J. Gorin, M. Roberts

captain and this became part of the articles of association in 1970. Previously one or two vice captains never succeeded to the captaincy. It is not unknown for there to be a ballot for the position of both vice captain and president, and this situation remains to the present day.

Interesting to ladies is the fact that originally the articles stated that at least one member of the committee should be a lady. The words "at least" were removed, leaving the wording "one of whom should be a lady". At the same time it was decided that the ladies' captain should be co–opted to serve on the general committee. A resolution by Mr. Chandler that ladies should not have the vote at AGMs was defeated, thus leaving Broadway one of the few truly democratic clubs and perpetuating the wishes of the founder members who clearly stated that ladies were on an equal footing with the men.

Sixth Period, 1950–62

1954, EGM regarding poor standard of the course called by eleven members.

1956, Mr. Rayner Booth resigned.

1957, first telephone installed.

1957, further mention of extending to 18 holes.

1957, general committee to have ladies' captain as co-opted member.

1961, first official vice captain appointed (J. R. Gorin).

1962, new nine holes opened April 21st.

Chapter Seven

Optimism Re-established 1962–74

The Clubhouse, Next Phase

OVER the years different things had dominated the deliberations of the officials and committee of Broadway Golf Club, perhaps the least of these being golf itself but certainly the clubhouse can take pole position. It was to be the origin of much emotion and strong opinions right up to the present day.

In 1958 whilst the new nine holes was being considered, although it was realised the facilities were inadequate, not everything could be done at the same time and the matter was given low priority. By 1960 the question of improvements to the clubhouse could be shelved no longer. The improvement plan was to be carried out in two parts, but in the main meant enlargement and improvement of changing and toilet facilities, room for caddy cars and professional's shop and workshop. The whole scheme would cost £1,000. Mr. George Knight was to deal with the matter. In hindsight it seems like money thrown away (improving old sheds) but who was to realise in 1960 that by 1965 the committee would be considering limiting membership to 500. Discussion continued. In 1962 Mr. Chandler was stating that the aim was to provide a clubhouse worthy of an 18-hole course. There was a suggestion of inaugurating a building fund. Should the improvements be by extension or new buildings? Was accommodation for staff necessary? Perhaps a building near the Dormy still owned by the club could be converted. It went on ad nauseam, the situation still being stalemate in September, 1963. It was left to Dr. Juckes to make a realistic statement that although the course had improved "the clubhouse remained as it had been for many years, no more than a tin shack". However was relief at hand? In September 1963, under the new Physical Training and Recreation Act a grant of 50 per cent towards a new building might be available and at an EGM the notion was to put up an entirely new clubhouse and apply for the grant. The work of processing the application was done by Bonzo Roberts, again giving his legal expertise free of charge. The cost of the scheme would be around £16,000 and the shortfall after the grant (supposing it were

96

given) would have to be made up by subscriptions which would have to go up 50 per cent making the top rate $13\frac{1}{2}$ guineas. Unfortunately the plans which were drawn for this stone building are not to be found but Keith Gilbert believes it was to be cantilevered over the Willersey quarry.

Was the problem of the clubhouse solved? The answer is no. In July 1965 the Chancellor of the Exchequer announced a cut-back in public spending and all grants were suspended. Yet an inspector visited and indicated the club would qualify but would have to wait for lifting of restrictions which would be at least six months. Remember it was by now seven years since realisation of the pressing need for a new clubhouse began to dawn. Congestion in the old "sheds" was becoming serious. Forty members took part in the Captains v Presidents match and had the greatest difficulty in gathering in the clubhouse after the game. The situation could only worsen. Membership of the club had risen to 470 and interest in golf was still increasing country-wide. Labour costs were rising and even if a 50 per cent grant were eventually allowed, the remainder would be more difficult to raise. Decision time had definitely arrived. The length of time procrastinating meant there was no choice. The plan for a complete new permanent building was abandoned and a proposal carried to erect the "system built" clubhouse

Interior of new clubhouse 1966

which many people remember, consisting of lounge, bar, kitchen and dining room, maximum cost £4,000. The new clubhouse was officially opened on November 12th, 1966 with an exhibition match given by Michael Lunt, English Amateur Champion and Lewine Guermont, English Ladies International. Ironically a grant of £7,500 had been offered towards a new permanent building but the committee were not prepared to change the decision. There could be valid arguments both ways as to whether this decision was correct but the matter had to be decided according to the conditions prevailing at the time. The feeling was that system building was the way of the future. The "experts" anticipated 50 years of useful life from the constructions, but failed to anticipate the amount of money needed to keep these buildings in good condition. The £4,000 was definitely not a finite figure – as will be shown later. However it is understandable that the committee and members in 1966 were highly delighted with the new facility as it was so vastly superior to what they had before. It meant that, for the first time, catering could be undertaken in the club's own facilities. At last the connection with the Dormy House could be severed. But what on the one hand was an advantage, on the other brought the committee the extra responsibility of finding satisfactory catering staff to provide food for members of all tastes, at a reasonable price – never an easy task.

Opening the bar, new clubhouse, 12th November 1966. George Knight (right) and Fred Harvey serving champagne

MEMBERSHIP AND SUBSCRIPTIONS

In 1963 the membership stood as follows:

> Men   193   Ladies   72   Total 265
> (New members 60, resigned 15).

By 1965 the ladies section had grown to 120 members and the overall club membership was approximately 460.

It was decided to increase the entrance fee to 7 guineas and increase the country membership distance to 25 miles.

Attempts had been made to raise the subscription over the past few years only to be defeated (last increase 1959). There was anxiety when the club was applying for the building grant because it was said if the subscription rose over £10 this would nullify the application. By 1966 this was history and money for the building scheme was raised through subscriptions.

March, 1966 – Subscriptions

Men	full members	14 guineas
	country members	7 guineas
Ladies	full members	9 guineas
	country members	$4\frac{1}{2}$ guineas
Clergy		9 guineas
Social		1 guinea
Junior (under 18)		1 guinea
	(over 18 male)	$4\frac{1}{2}$ guineas
	(over 18 female)	3 guineas

Keith Gilbert did research into the "clergy" category of membership when he was captain. It appeared that at its best there were two members but this was reduced to one! This was the priest at Campden Roman Catholic Church who reckoned to arrive for his game approximately ten minutes after Sunday morning mass. The trend was becoming firmly established upwards and this was only the start of clubhouse development, but the AGM of 1967 showed how interest was being maintained with an attendance at the meeting of 146 full paying members as well as the officers.

FORWARD PLANNING

With an 18-hole course and improved clubhouse, costs were rising. At the AGM in 1967, the treasurer pointed out that the profit of £680 was not sufficient to cover commitments. The clubhouse was a drain on resources: the lounge needed new fittings; the old lounge had been changed to part office, part ladies room. But these changes were meant to be only temporary as the committee had plans for extending the new lounge with men's changing rooms, ladies changing rooms and new offices. The old professional's shop had been pulled down to make way for the new lounge and had to be replaced with another shed.

At this time also, the idea was mooted for an automatic watering system on the greens. It was also essential the electricity supply be changed to three phase and the car park needed extending.

Indeed the requirement for capital expenditure was never ending. Extremes of opinion vied with each other (and continued to do so for years). There were those who wanted to do all improvements now and at the other end of the scale those who wished for a halt on spending. Four alternatives were put forward at the meeting (1967) with four new subscription rates, 17, 20, 22 and 24 guineas. These were rates for men with all other subscriptions

99

pro rata. The amount of work possible on the income was likewise scaled from nothing to everything. In the end the first proposal was carried which meant that improvements to the course and clubhouse would be brought to a standstill but would ensure a reasonable profit to cover rising costs and the repayment of the bank loan which stood at £3,300.

A very important step was taken at this point (1967), a step which it is probably true to say has kept the club solvent to the present day. Right up to his death in 1963 at the age of 85, Mr. Rayner Booth the hon. sec. had been the dominant influence. Attempts had been made in the past to adopt a more professional approach but as the club was becoming bigger business, a further tightening up of management was necessary and for this reason the Finance and General Purpose Committee was set up. The main purpose of this was to plan budgets in order to avoid runaway costs as seemed to have been the danger after the new lounge was built, and to eliminate the constant worry about finances.

FURTHER CLUBHOUSE EXPENSES

In 1969 new men's changing rooms were an essential improvement, to be built at a cost of £5,500. An EGM was called for October 4th, 1971 – the agenda "alteration to the clubhouse". The captain Mr. M. J. Steward spoke of the development over the past years but now the club had reached a stage where there was a waiting list for membership. Dining facilities were not large enough, especially when visiting teams were being catered for, the ladies' rooms and secretary's office were in a bad state. The proposal was to extend the lounge on the south side to give a larger dining and kitchen area, move the bar to the western side of the lounge, build ladies' rooms, provide a trolley store and build a secretary's office. The cost was to be £12,000, the work to be completed by the spring by Charles Steward and Son, who had built the new lounge. The actual cost was £11,000, finance provided by members' loans within a range of £10 to a maximum of £420.

One question from the floor at this meeting concerned more substantial building but the general consensus was that system building would meet needs and be quite adequate for the foreseeable future. The club had prided itself on being a self-help society, members provided free labour and lent money at low interest rates. Thus people were very personally involved; opinions were subjective. After the 1971 improvements, things were quiet on the clubhouse front for a few years only to restart as ferociously as ever when the provision of a more permanent building began to be mooted in 1977. Around £21,000 had been spent on sectional buildings which no one had anticipated replacing for 50 years.

Clubhouse from 17th Tee

1st green

2nd green looking towards 2nd tee

5th hole

6th green

7th hole

9th green

9th and 18th green

11th green

12th hole

13th green

14th hole

15th green

16th

17th tee

18th green

THE COURSE AND GOLF

During this decade Frank Bisgrove, who came to the club on a three month's trial in the early 1920s, reached retiring age. At the AGM February, 1963, the president, Mr. Gardiner, made a presentation, mentioning how the club was indebted to him for his long and faithful service and Bisgrove was made an honorary life member. The honour was of little use to him as he returned to his west country roots at Burnham, where he lived in a residential home until his death in June, 1988. The proprietor of the home, a Mrs. Popham, tells us that "he was always talking golf, and was very proud of the days when he was a professional for 40 years". Mr. Rayner Booth, with whom Bisgrove had had such a long association, had died in the previous January; Mr. Dalrymple had resigned as honorary secretary and Mr. Gardiner finished his term as president – it was the end of another era. But there is always someone to be found to fill a gap and this time it was John Freeman. John had been a professional since 1945. At 14 he was an assistant to George Maisey at the Robin Hood Club, Birmingham, where he stayed (except for National Service) until 1954 when he became professional/greenkeeper at Droitwich. In 1962 he went abroad to the Vienna Golf Club and finally in 1963 taking Bisgrove's place at Broadway,

becoming professional/green-keeper. John has always been a teacher at heart rather than a competitive player and many golfers both local and world wide have had cause to be grateful for his knowledge and patience. He also has a remarkable memory for names and faces. Under the new regime keenness and interest in the game flourished.

Frank Bisgrove's retirement presentation.
L to r: F. Bisgrove, J. Gorin, C. Gardiner, W.D. Dalrymple

In 1963 Mr. G. Chandler played for the Gloucester County team. The reputation which has survived for George Chandler is that he was a formidable opponent. To prevent the opposition knowing which club he was using, word has it that he never put the correct head cover on his clubs!

Mr. Roberts (Bonzo) was elected vice president of the Gloucestershire Golf Union. Over the years Mr. Roberts had been tireless in his work for the club up to his death in 1978.

It was in 1963 that a B team for men was first discussed, becoming formed in the following year. The men's A team had played 18 matches, won 11, lost 5 and halved 2.

In 1966 A. G. Chandler and T. R. L. Gorin played in the county second team whilst Miss Jenny Foxon was chosen for the ladies' county team, to be joined two years later by Miss Price.

Fred Prosser with Ferguson tractor

The greens were flourishing under John Freeman, resulting in excellent playing conditions. Several new sand bunkers were made; as much machinery as possible was acquired in order to help the small labour force. Fred Prosser had been employed for the course in 1960 and Hilda Prosser for the clubhouse. This lady was a "treasure" to the club. She kept the buildings spick and span, and took pride in looking after the welfare of members. Apparently her Eccles cakes were famed – better than anything seen before or since (according to Keith Gilbert). Perhaps the same cannot be said of her tea, which Les Arnold tells was made in a large army type pot which she kept topping up until it became well and truly stewed. To quote Les, "We dare not say a word as it was better than nothing and we did not like to upset the old dear."

The top of Willersey Hill, being rather bleak, is not a natural habitat for trees and a planting programme was put in hand. Mr. Les Arnold planted the trees alongside the 17th fairway, now known as Arnold's Copse but later years have seen many more, often having to be protected by a leylandii hedge until established. Four hundred were planted in 1965 alone, and the programme has continued to the present day.

The original layout of the new nine was kept but there was room for improvement. The 1st green was altered in 1965, a new 12th green was made in 1967, followed by a new 18th green – cost, £401. The "snake pit" by the 13th green was bought from Group 4 for £50 in exchange for permission to connect the water supply from the Dormy House to Farncombe. This made possible improvements to the 11th tee. Starting boards were introduced, the car park enlarged and an extra greenkeeper employed. In 1970 a new 6th tee was made, thus avoiding congestion on the 5th, because of players waiting for the old 6th tee to clear before driving off. An extension was built to the 8th green, taking it further back up a bank.

The trophy count was increasing. In 1964 the Stanley Bowl and the Harvey Cup were presented. In 1968 the Rummer Cup was given by a visiting golfer from Holland. Mrs. Alex Jeffrey donated a silver salver in 1973 in memory of her husband. This has been played as a mixed competition with a handicap limit.

The North Gloucestershire Foursomes League was played for the first time and in 1969 it was won by the Broadway team. When Broadway were successful the competition was played under handicap. After Broadway won, the then "major" clubs voted at the next annual meeting to change the format to scratch.

The first pro-am was played in 1973. This was very popular in the beginning and became one of the highlights of the golfing year. It was first of all organised by the club but the PGA took over and this restricted the area from which the professionals could be drawn and the prize money available was not sufficient to attract top class pros. Members became disenchanted and this, coupled with the start of the recession, meant the death knell of the competition. The last one was held in 1991.

North Gloucestershire Foursome League, winning team 1969, l to r: D. Gisbourne, G. Woodger, G. Chandler, J. Gorin, R. Denison, A. Hughes, R. Gash, J. Steward, A. Jeffrey, C. Price

The course was obviously becoming busier so a resolution was passed that there should be no visiting societies at weekends or Bank Holidays. A point of interest: in 1968 the rule was laid down that whilst ladies were allowed in the clubhouse on Sundays they could not play on the course before noon. For many years ladies were under the misapprehension that the clubhouse also was sacrosanct but this was challenged and corrected two or three years ago! In 1970 it was first agreed that Ladies' Day should be officially Wednesday (later changed to Tuesday).

Noteworthy achievements continued in the 1970s. Tony Holt won the Stratford Town Bowl; Keith Gilbert won the Red Horse Open competition at Stratford in 1970; Cliff Price won the Shakespeare Cup; Nigel Robinson became Gloucestershire Junior Champion; Tim Gorin, Jenny Foxon and Ann Short all played for county teams.

In 1972 the captain, Mr. Tony Short had changed the order of play, making the present 17th the 1st, 18th the 2nd, then there was a move round to the present 10th, and the first nine finished on the present 16th. This meant that players could then approach the next tee (the present 1st) across the car park instead of crossing the fairway. Play could be speeded up generally. However the change proved very unpopular, causing a split in the membership. Some people thought the change was made dictatorially. The following year the course reverted to the old order of play, but the idea was not laid to rest, becoming contentious again in 1977, but once more defeated.

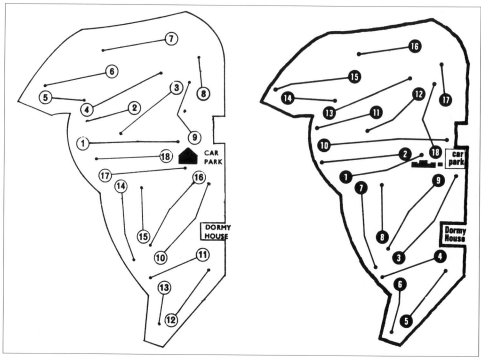

Original order of play　　　　　　　　　　　　　*Changed order of play for 1972 season*

AN AUTOMATIC WATERING SYSTEM

On December 4th, 1972 an EGM was called to consider the installation of an automatic watering system. Mr. John Walker, greens committee chairman, explained how the original nine was still watered through the old metal pipes and the new nine by polythene which could not be repaired easily. The modern method of watering was for it to be done automatically at night using pop-up sprinklers on every green supplied by water from a reservoir filled from the mains. Fairways and tees could be watered from take-off points. The Water Board could supply 10,000 gallons an hour against a demand for 6,000 gallons a night, an ample supply. The club was very lucky to have a 2" mains supply, the usual being $\frac{3}{4}$". Cost would be £8,100. The bankers were ready to extend overdraft facilities and it was hoped extra green fees plus bar profits would make up any shortfall of cash.

Apart from the officials, the 91 members present all voted in favour – except one, identity unknown!

Coupled with the modernisation of the watering system, perhaps one of the most important developments in 1973 was the employment of Mr. Cedric Gough as head greenkeeper. Cedric was brought from Ross-on-Wye Golf Club and worked under the direction of Mr. John Walker for a number

---

J.H. Arthur B.Sc.(Agric.)   22nd July 1976

Little Garth, Charlton, Banbury, Oxon OX17 3DP. Tel: Kings Sutton 318

Dr. W.M.Savery,
Captain,
Broadway Golf Club,
Wiiersey Hill, Broadway.

Dear Dr. Savery,

Thank you for your letter of the 15th JJuly and your thanks for my past
advice. I obviously regret the severing of an advisory connection with
Broadway, going back to the days of Rayner Booth, immediately after the
war, and which has been continuous for the past twelve years, but no
specialist can continue to advise a patient who throws his prescriptions
down the sink and uses something different, as I am sure you will be
the first to agree.

I am sorry to see Broadway apparently committed to the current vogue for
soft lush greens, but if at any time situations arise where you, or your
successor, may feel that a return to the policies which I have unswervingly
advocated for nearly thirty years, might be helpful, please do not hesitate
to get in touch with me. Cedric is a good youngster but obviously
as yet too inexperienced to stand up to an assault by members who want
something different from those conditions which those of us with deeper
roots in golf than the current 'generation' regard as the ideal to aim at.

Yours sincerely,

Agronomist to the Championship Committee, Royal & Ancient Golf Club of St. Andrews

---

Cedric has proved himself well able to withstand any assault by members

of years. Greens committees come and go but over the past 22 years it is mainly Cedric's expertise that has shaped the course, making Broadway's greens some of the best and trickiest in the area and causing one visiting TV celebrity, Lance Percival, when playing a charity function in 1989 to comment in his speech, "Of course your head greenkeeper is a practical joker!" Eventually a house was bought for Cedric at South Littleton, which he later purchased from the club.

SENIORS SECTION

The seniors section was formed in 1968 by a group of senior golfers led by Frank Davis, and has gradually grown in popularity to the present day. This small band met together early on Mondays, Wednesdays and Fridays in the car park, where they drew for partners for their four ball games.

The first captain of the seniors was Mr. J. A. Reynolds. He held the post for three years, and gave the trophy which bears his name. It was the first competition limited to senior golfers. Today this trophy is competed for annually and entry is by qualification in an 18-hole medal, the top 16 going forward in a knock-out to win the trophy.

The section played its first match against Moor Hall in March, 1971, winning by seven games to one. In 1985 a second trophy was added, presented by Mr. Mark Booth and is described as a "Battered old tankard". Any player over 70 is given one point for each year. It was instigated to give a trophy to these, "Poor old chaps who can't hit a ball very far in their dotage", yet many chaps in their 80s play a full round and return some very good scores.

The Martin Sumpner Rose Bowl was donated in 1988. This is a knock-out competition, competed for annually by 64 golfers, always oversubscribed.

By this time the section had grown to some 65 members, all retired, all over 60 and most playing regularly three days a week. A great camaraderie had grown up, not only on the course but in the 19th, as well as among wives.

Match numbers increased to eight home, and eight away, plus one each against the ladies and juniors. They could never beat the juniors but the ladies never won until a trophy was presented at which point the ladies pulled their socks up and have won every time since!

Seniors 1973, standing l to r: –. Denison, unknown, C. Lamb, A. Knight, unknown, unknown, M. Sumpner, F. Davis. Sitting l to r: F. Harvey, W. English, B. Dearnley, –. Law

The seniors continued to grow in numbers, almost 80 playing regularly, and in 1990 winter friendly competitions were started. After each competition the captain had the job of cutting the handicaps of the winner by 10 per cent, the second by 5 per cent and the third by 1 per cent depending on the score – always great fun.

A trophy was presented in 1991 by Mr. Laurie Wolder, to be played for in pairs on two separate days, the aggregate of the two scores to win the trophy – again always fully subscribed.

1994 saw an official constitution for the seniors, and every male member over the age of 60 is now automatically a member of the section. In 1993 the seniors organised their first Open Day.

In fact, it seems that if any player wants to continue playing 18 holes until he is 90, the answer is, "Join Broadway Golf Club".

Seventh Period, 1962–74

1963, death of Mr. Booth – January 6th aged 85.

1963, EGM November 12th re a new clubhouse – no decision.

1963, Frank Bisgrove retires. John Freeman arrives.

1964, EGM new clubhouse approved.

1965, plans for £20,000 permanent building with help of government grant – plan abandoned.

1966, system built clubhouse for £4,000 opened November 12th.

1966, first full-time caterer, Miss Pauline Albutt.

1967, old quarry by 13th green bought.

1967, five-day membership introduced.

1967, first finance and general purposes sub committee.

1967, limit on membership – 500 full and country members (outside 25 miles) plus 50 social members.

1968, North Glos. Foursomes League played for first time.

1968, seniors section started.

1969, new men's changing room, cost £5,500.

1970, first agreed ladies' day – Wednesdays.

1972, EGM December 4th, first automatic watering system approved – 91 for, 1 against – cost £8,100.

1973, arrival of head greenkeeper, Mr. Cedric Gough.

1973, first pro-am.

Chapter Eight

Approaching Modern Times
1974–82

DECISION TIME AGAIN

EVEN after all these years the club was not able to forget the Dormy House and its attendant problems. Both the Dormy and Farncombe were now owned by Group 4. It was definitely to the advantage of the Dormy House to be able to purchase land by the 11th green and the club could certainly use the money – they had in mind provision of a new steel-framed greenkeeper's shed.

Unfortunately some acrimony seems to have entered the business discussions. The owners had the benefit of three covenants in place from years ago when the land was first bought from Captain Butler. They were prepared to sell two (involving a right of way from the Dormy House to the quarry by the 13th) by reducing the proposed purchase price of £15,000 by £1,000 but wanted to enforce the right of guests at Farncombe House to play on the course without payment (the same covenant which Mr. Pemberton had sought to implement). The matter was not settled until 1979 when it was agreed that Farncombe House was a business and no longer had any bona fide guests. The club had bought the land behind the 14th tee from Group 4 for £50 in 1976, enabling this tee and the 11th to be enlarged. Altogether the transactions had taken five years to complete.

GENERAL FINANCES

From 1976 the finances of the club were taken over by Mr. Keith Gilbert and Mr. David Senior, an accountant by profession, and they were instrumental in keeping the resources on a very tight rein, no doubt remembering that after the opening of the new clubhouse in 1966 expenses nearly got out of hand. The budgetary planning of Mr. Gilbert and Mr. Senior was to take the club into the strong financial position of being able to rebuild in 1988.

In the 1970s rising costs were making themselves felt and in 1975 it was deemed necessary to raise both entrance fees and subscriptions – men £45, ladies £30 (inclusive of VAT which then stood at 8 per cent) from £30 and

£20 respectively. The trend upwards continued annually due to the general rising inflation. However, in spite of this, Mr. Senior was able to state in 1977 that "our subs were the lowest in Gloucestershire, except one".

The rise in subscriptions was slightly mitigated for members over 65 who had belonged to the club for ten years. They were given a 25 per cent reduction. As costs have risen, this was changed to £25 and a proposal to abolish the privilege altogether was defeated at the AGM in 1994 after an eloquent plea by Mr. Ken Marshall, the seniors' captain. Green fees were raised in 1980 from £5 to £6 weekdays, and £7.50 to £8.50 weekends – still comparatively cheap golf. But inflation had forced the pay of the greenkeepers up 23 per cent and Willersey Parish Council put a heavy increase on the rent they charged for the part of the car park they owned (i.e. by the right of the gateway). The club have failed in all attempts to buy this piece of land. In fact the sale of the quarry by Willersey Parish Council would require an Act of Parliament!

GOLF AND THE COURSE

The enthusiasm which recommenced in the late 1950s continued unabated. In 1975 the Ladies' County Championship was held at Broadway for the first time when Miss Jenny Foxon was defeated in the final. Mark Swain won the Gloucester Junior Championship in 1977. In 1979 Broadway ladies finished first in the Gloucester League and two years' later the men's team won promotion from Division two to Division one. Amount of play was increasing to such an extent that in 1980 there were 180 entries for the Tilbrook Cup. Most competitions were so oversubscribed that numbers had to be reduced by handicap limits. In the 1970s and 1980s, as now, there was concern over the number of outside matches played and there was talk of reduction. The compromise was that matches were restricted to 12 a side.

All the time improvements continued to be made on the course. In 1974 the 14th green was rebuilt, eliminating the slope towards the wall, and in 1979 a new 13th, at an estimated cost of £515 and £1,700 respectively. Remeasuring took place in 1976 – the old length was 6,129 yards. The greatest discrepancy was on the 9th which was changed from 416 yards to 349 yards; this was still found to be wrong and eventually settled at 410 yards, making the total for the course 6,211 yards. The stroke index was changed to that now used.

After much deliberation, approval was given in 1981 to cut two holes per green to give a "new" weekend hole. An improved 1st tee was considered necessary as it was dangerous to drive off the tee in the corner by the car park (now used sometimes in winter) when players were on the 9th green.

DRIVING RANGE AND RELIEF CAR PARK

At the AGM in 1980 the renting of a piece of land from Mr. Michael Webb was first mentioned. For many years the professional, John Freeman, and his pupils had braved the winds which in winter whistle over the practice ground, parallel to the 17th fairway, one of the highest points on the course. The plan was to erect a couple of sheds, with mats, in the field directly opposite as well as marking distances off down the field. As playing membership increased the need for further car-parking space was becoming obvious. It was hoped to use part of the field as a relief car park. Arrangements were finally concluded. The practice area and car park were opened in 1984. Both have proved a definite asset to the club as well as to the professional who is able to loan the balls – large or small baskets depending on how great is the need or how much energy is to spare.

JUNIORS

Juniors were mentioned in the archives of Broadway Golf Club way back in the 1920s. At this time the term did not mean youngsters, but players who were new at the game. This fell into disuse and the term was used as we know it today. Although young people were admitted they were not organised into a junior section until 1974, by Wing-Commander Frank Tams. Frank Tams had been captain in 1972. He became president in 1978 to 1981 and president of the Gloucestershire County Golf Union in 1984, thus following in the footsteps of Dr. W. G. Alexander in 1932 and Mr. H. Osbourne Roberts in 1964. Wing-Commander Tams continued to run the section until 1981 when Mr. Les Carter took over, and stood in again in 1986 until 1990 when Mr. George Sloggett (also ex captain and president) expressed himself willing to take on the job.

Junior "Opens" were organised by county clubs when a close watch was kept for promising players who could be coached for the county team. Standards were so high that Duncan Singer (Frank Tam's grandson) failed to be selected for the county team with a handicap of 4! This boy became club champion in 1979 and 1980 at the age of 15, won the Lloyd Cup in 1979 and the under 14 Midlands prize at Blackwell. David Fletcher played for the county team and was captain for one year to be followed by Mark Dove. Both David and Mark won the club championship three times each; Mark won the Lloyd Cup as a junior in 1987. Both eventually turned pro. Frank Tams says that during his period as organiser of the juniors he was fortunate in having a group of boys who all reduced their handicaps through hard work, sometimes playing 36 or even 54 holes a day. This still prevails today when the dedication of most of these young boys can only be admired. A junior, Robert Lane, took first prize on Captain's Day in Centenary Year, and young

Matthew Miller had a hole in one – believed to be the first junior to do so. It is a pity that more girls do not join them. Some of the best players in the club started as juniors – Mark Swain (tragically killed), Shaun Thornhill, John Richmond, Mark Leary as well as John Freeman's son, Martyn, now the professional himself.

1977, three young champions with John Freeman. From left: M. Freeman, M. Swain, J. Freeman, D. Singer

THE CLUBHOUSE

In the mid 1970s, the clubhouse once more took centre stage. A building committee was formed and a firm of local architects, Badger, Harrison and Cross, was employed to draw up plans. The idea was to re-clad the temporary building with outside walls and slate roof. Extensions were to include a snooker room and steward's accommodation. The estimated cost was £165,000. When the plans were exhibited for members perusal, they brought forth a plethora of adverse criticism, the main one being that the proposed building was far too elaborate. In the event no vote was taken as opinion was obvious. The plan was abandoned but in 1979 at an EGM "an extension to clubhouse – new beer cellar plus extension to lounge bar area at a cost not exceeding £18,000" was passed, 54 votes to 20. By this time membership stood at around 600.

As late as 1980 the clubhouse was still absorbing money like a sponge. The new building work was almost completed (i.e. new cellar and spike bar). But it is quite obvious that a new cellar was essential as the old one was totally inadequate, being only three to four feet high, awkward and dangerous. Crates had to be stored outside, a nuisance and an eyesore. Repairs to the roof (which was felt) cost approximately £1,500, and a new boiler and ducting £1,396. There was also talk of extending the dining room. Long-term plans both for the building and means of raising funds were essential and the task was undertaken by Mr. David Senior and a small committee. By 1981 a more permanent clubhouse was mentioned for the first time by Mr. Senior, on publishing that the income over expenditure had been £12,081, well over what was budgeted. The directors felt that "This windfall profit should be used to plan towards the probable need of replacing the club-house, since the original building is only of a "temporary nature". Those who had opposed system building were being proved correct. Professional advice was sought by the building committee from Mr. David Renfrew FRICS (whose grandfather had been a founder member). At a building committee meeting on April 15th, 1982, three options were discussed:

1. Continue and maintain the existing structure – cost £7,000 p.a. excluding improvements.
2. Upgrade the existing structure at 1981 prices from Badger, Harrison and Cross at £170,000. This would cause considerable disruption.
3. Build new.

It was agreed by the building committee that to build new was the best option, to aim for ten years hence at an approximate cost of £250,000 at 1982 prices. In the interim the existing building must be maintained. The club was in a healthy financial position and the committee felt that now the clubhouse was more important than the course.

An EGM was called on September 10th, 1982; the resolution was "that provision be made in the 1982/83 budget and in subsequent years' budgets to build a new clubhouse within approximately 10 years at an estimated cost of £250,000 at current prices".

After thorough discussion the resolution was heavily defeated, 102 votes against, only 45 in favour.

SPECIAL RESOLUTION

At the AGM on October 22nd, 1979, the committee, concerned at rumours appertaining to the sale of the club to outside agencies, put forward a special resolution. This resolution asked the meeting to change the memo-randum of association by adding a clause that 75 per cent of all full members would have to approve the sale of lands etc. as opposed to 75 per cent of members (including proxy votes) who actually attend an AGM or EGM. The vote was 45 members in favour of the resolution and 25 against and as this was short of the required 75 per cent the resolution was defeated.

This result caused some surprise as all those who spoke at the meeting urged acceptance and many were under the misapprehension that a simple majority was all that was required.

It is a fact that it has proved in the past almost impossible to reach 75 per cent of those attending meetings to make any changes to the constitution of the club which in any way could be considered controversial. Even today this position is not fully appreciated.

EIGHTH PERIOD, 1974–82

1974, Dormy House yard sold for £14,000.
1974, 14th green re-built.
1974, house purchased for greenkeeper.
1976, land behind 14th tee bought for £50.
1976, plans for major extensions to clubhouse abandoned.
1978, Mr. Ken Lawrance appointed as secretary, April 1st.
1978, Bonzo Roberts dies.
1979, EGM March 2nd, extensions to clubhouse approved – cost £18,000.
1979, Special resolution to change memorandum of association defeated.
1980, building committee set up to investigate long term plans.
1980, land leased for driving and relief car park.
1981, system of two holes per green approved.
1982, EGM September 10th, plan to provide a building fund for a new permanent clubhouse by raising £250,000 over ten years rejected.

Chapter Nine

Building for the Future
1982–95

A New Clubhouse

ONLY three years later, Mr. Michael Webb, the retiring captain, stated in his report "the extent of emergency repairs meant the prepared maintenance programme had to be abandoned".

It is not surprising therefore that yet another EGM was called on September 22nd, 1986 to discuss the building of a new clubhouse. The attendance was good; 169 full members were present. The captain, Mr. S. E. Clews, mentioned the research done at other clubs who had embarked on a building programme, and hoped that members would support the project. Mr. Don Palmer, himself a past captain, in the building trade for many years, spoke on the need for a permanent building. The estimate was that around £100,000 would have to be spent on maintenance and renewals in the present clubhouse. Indeed the professional's shop was little more than a shed, vulnerable to thieves. The kitchen was unsatisfactory. The changing facilities old fashioned – all this in spite of the large amount of money which had already been spent.

The building committee invited six architects to produce a scheme, four responded and all recommended demolition of the existing building. The committee had selected the scheme of the Broad and Bennett partnership. Mr. Broad was present at the meeting and presented the scheme in great detail with the aid of slides. Mr. Keith Gilbert spoke on the financial aspects with suggestions for raising money. Eventually it was agreed to offer subscriptions at a reduced rate if any member was prepared to pay five years in advance. The overall saving to the member would be about 12 per cent. A rise in subscriptions was proposed: 1987 – £160, 1988 – £180, 1989 – £200, as well as the doubling of entry fees to twice the annual subscription (payable in two equal parts). Of course numerous questions were asked regarding the financial aspect – overdraft facilities and so on. Mr. David Senior said "the Club's financial status attracted overdraft facilities. Early in the year a high credit balance is available". He also pointed out that the club's reserves would be eaten away if it was decided to maintain the present

114

building, "not much of a legacy for future generations of the club". Discussion ranged through size of lounge, double glazing, trolley store, lockers, security. A very pertinent comment was made by Mr. Steward (a past captain). He referred back to many years ago when the membership rejected a stone building for £17,000 with a £3 increase in subscriptions. "They dodged the issue then, we must not dodge it again". The opposing opinion is perhaps summed up by the comment, "We will get a millstone round our necks". The resolution was carried quite narrowly 143 votes for, 104 voted against. It was estimated the whole cost would not exceed £350,000.

Planning procedures had to be put in hand, and at first permission was withheld. A group of archaeologists had to undertake a dig to make sure that the proposed site of the new building would not be disturbing the Iron Age monument. But difficulties were ironed out and building work began in early November, 1987. By August, 1988 it was necessary to call another EGM because it had become apparent that the original sum of

1985, interior of system built clubhouse

£350,000 was insufficient. Mr. Palmer explained that about one hundred variations to the original bills of quantity had been requested by the committee! Extra items of furnishing had not been allowed for as well as replacement of cooker and dishwasher which it was decided were worn out. Certain items were "in dispute" with the contractors and architect and "too delicate" to discuss. But why spoil the ship for a ha'porth of tar? When asked to state how much would be required in round figures, Mr. Senior stated £62,000; the meeting approved the additional expenditure by a large majority, only two votes being recorded against. The meeting was informed that the secretary's office and professional's shop would be moved between September 2nd and 4th. The main move would be carried out during the weekend 10/11th and demolition of the old (but not so old!) building would begin September 12th.

So the end was in sight. Right through early planning, rejection, further planning and acceptance stages, Broadway Golf Club is heavily indebted to Mr. Don Palmer for the tremendous amount of time and effort he gave to ensure the project was completed as smoothly as possible.

It was decided to hold a party to mark the demolition – the last in the old place – it was a good party but rather sad for some members who had been involved from the beginning. Fancy dress "Tramps and Vamps" was the

1988, old and new standing together

order of the day and a surprising number of sedate people let their hair down. Mr. Tony Gisbourne was surely straight off stage from *Waiting for Godot,* whilst we discovered that the building committee had been organised and financially advised by a precocious St. Trinians school girl and a French maid!

OPENING CEREMONY

The new clubhouse was officially opened on October 1st, 1988 by Dr. David Marsh, president of the English Golf Union. A marble plaque to commemorate the occasion was donated by Mr. Stan Linley and placed on the stairway where the opening ceremony took place. A pleasant social day was enjoyed by all wishing to attend, buffet and wine being available until stocks were finished. A dance was held in the evening for the benefit of the livelier members.

1988, opening ceremony (October 1st) performed by Dr. D.M. Marsh, president of the English Golf Union with his wife (far left). Mr. & Mrs. Gilbert (president), Mrs. P. Young (lady captain), Mr. A.T. Godfrey (captain) and Mrs. Godfrey

1988, topping out ceremony. Centre front: A.T. Godfrey (captain) with J. Skinner (Meades of Evesham Ltd). Front row left: architects Broad and Bennett. Front row right: K.S. Lawrance, club secretary

116

NEW BUILDING IN USE

The new clubhouse itself, now seven years old, is now there for all to see and continues to be a topic for comment and discussion. As might be anticipated a few things needed modification when the building was put into use, the most important being the incorporation of the visitors' changing room into the men's which were proving inadequate. However in 1994 plans were drawn up and planning permission obtained to enlarge the main room by covering in one of the balconies to make a separate dining room – the cost was estimated to be £60–£70,000. This plan was abandoned. It was certainly unpopular with the membership who could not see the need to spend so much, so soon, on a new building.

Outside the architecture of the building blends well with the surroundings and is aesthetically pleasing. The landscaping of the disturbed ground as well as the site of the old clubhouse has been expertly carried out by Mr. Cedric Gough and his team as well as the re-laying of the putting green – all extra to the usual work on the course. To quote the captain of the day, "It is not generally appreciated just how much work the greens staff got through, and not always under perfect conditions."

CAR PARK

The old car park had not been enhanced by its use by heavy building vehicles and was in need of complete replanning. Mr. Oliver Dicks was largely responsible for the organisation and supervision of this work. Mr. Dicks's experience as a building inspector was invaluable to the club over the re-building years when he served on various building committees and gave them the benefit of his professional advice.

FIRST ANNUAL BALL IN THE NEW BUILDING

Apart from the opening ceremony, the first official function to be held in the new clubhouse was the Annual Ball, 1988. Broadway Golf Club had held an annual function almost from its inception, first of all just a dinner, and as membership increased a dinner and dance. Either the Lygon Arms and later the Dormy House Hotel had been the venue but with a new building the committee felt it should be used for this purpose. The first ball had to be a masterpiece of planning in order to fit in all who wished to attend, several layouts of tables and chairs being tried by the captain and vice captain. The problem was solved in later years by limiting numbers.

SPARKS CHARITY DAY – *Sports Aiding Research into Crippling Diseases*

An important function which filled the new clubhouse in the summer of 1989 was a charity day in aid of Sparks. Members were invited to enter teams of three at a cost of £300. Each team was then allotted a celebrity as a fourth member. Thirty teams were entered. The competition was a stableford, two scores to count, and was eventually won by Jim Cockerton's team with 97 points. The celebrities came from the world of sport and entertainment – people like Geoffrey Boycott, Michael Grade, Michael Parkinson to mention a few. All food was donated, and prepared by the chef of the Dormy House Hotel who took over the kitchen for the day. The Dormy House Hotel also provided the visitors with accommodation if required. A sum of £9,000 was raised for the charity, as well as all enjoying an excellent day's entertainment. The weather on the day was beautiful, Broadway course was at its best with the Malvern Hills and the Black Mountains of Wales stretching away hazily in the distance. Ann Robinson (of *Points of View* and *Watchdog* fame) commented on her radio programme that she had just visited a lovely place "on the top of the world" – Broadway Golf Club.

It was attempted to repeat the Sparks day in subsequent years but recession was beginning to grip and units of £300 to enter a golfing event were not so readily available and the attempts failed.

1989, Sparks Day for charity. Captains team l to r: F. Penny (captain), R. Cumper (vice captain), Michael Grade (head of Channel 4 TV), K. Gilbert (president)

GOLFING ACHIEVEMENTS

Obviously such a large rebuilding project had preoccupied the time and thoughts of the committee, meanwhile golf was continuing successfully.

1993, North Gloucestershire County Foursomes Div. 1 winners. Standing l to r: L. Carter, S. Keyte, J. Cockerton, J. O'Hagen, S. Thornhill, W. Barrett, M. Dove. Front row l to r: J. Richmond, S. Rainbow, A. Hedley, M. Humpston, J. Haines, J. Rainbow

Many achievements and outstanding players have already been mentioned. At the start of the hundred years it was easy to describe, standards were lower, numbers were less. But as the century moved on it has become more difficult to choose from the plethora of successes by both teams and individuals.

Mark Dove has been described as an outstanding junior and has gone from strength to strength. In 1988 he was selected to play for England boys in the European Championships and the Home International. In 1989, Mark (scratch) along with James Webber (+1 and comparative newcomer to the club), represented the county. The following year Mark Dove was second in the Lagonda, second in the Southport and Ainsdale Bowl and reached the quarter finals in the English Amateur Championship. Again, with James Webber, he was selected for England in the European Youth Team Championship in Italy – two of six players. Playing for England in a two man team in the French Nations Cup, Mark won by two shots from France. In 1991 James Webber became county champion and was subsequently third in the County Champions Tournament. The same year Mark Dove was once again in the England squad. As a professional Mark has entered a tough competitive world – the good wishes of Broadway Golf Club go with him.

One member who unfortunately has left the area, Tim Gorin, was one of the most successful players. From 1966 to 1981 he won the Club Championship nine times, an achievement nobody has matched since.

Miss Jenny Foxon's career has continued to flourish. She won the first ladies' club championship in 1982 and achieved the same honour no less than seven times more.

Tim Gorin

119

1982, Broadway Ladies carried off the Watson Williams Cup and the County Foursomes Trophy, l to r: J.M. Foxon, S. Aitkenhead, P.E. Samways, S.M. Stacey (lady captain), J. Gisbourne

1991, Lister Cup Winners, l to r: M. Humpston, J. Richmond, M. Dove, J. Webber

Also in 1982, Jenny and Mrs. Sheila Aitkenhead, won the Watson Williams Scratch Cup, repeating the performance in 1994 with Mrs. Linda Everitt. Three other ladies have held the Ladies Championship Trophy. Miss Henrietta Cooke who was the county ladies captain in 1989, Miss Lynne Chambers and Mrs. Sheila Aitkenhead. It seemed appropriate this summer that Miss Foxon should win the Ladies Centenary Trophy after such a long and successful association with Broadway Golf Club.

In 1982 Mr. Mike Humpston who had been playing professional golf was reinstated at Broadway as an amateur. In 1991 Mike Humpston, Mark Dove, James Webber and John Richmond were victors in the Lister Cup competition, the first time this trophy had come to Broadway.

In 1990 Mr. Arthur Gray, a former captain, won a national competition, the "Rover", thus qualifying for the next round at Royal Birkdale. Here he was successful again and went to La Manga, Spain, in October where the competition was held on Ryder Cup lines, between England, Ireland, Scotland, Wales.

A married couple who have probably won more of the club's mixed competitions than anyone else is Mr. and Mrs. Fred Powers (although this assumption could perhaps be disputed by Mr. and Mrs. Tony Gisbourne). Their crowning achievement came in 1991 when they won their way through to the final of the Douglas Bader competition at Turnbury.

An interesting precedent was set in 1991 when Paddy Sloane, John Salmon, Richard Jarvis and Stewart Hepburn were playing a friendly fourball as they had done many times before. They came to the 11th, a 285 yard par 4. Paddy shot a par, John a birdie 3, Richard an eagle 2, Stewart a hole-in-one! What are the odds against that one wonders.

WINTER LEAGUE

1995 is the 25th anniversary of the start of the Winter League. The number of men's monthly medals had been steadily reduced over the years until by 1969 they were down to four a year. John Walker and Keith Gilbert felt there needed to be a reason to get more members on the course at weekends and they decided to organise the Winter League, at first a casual affair but which has now become an official club competition.

The initial format was eight rounds of four betterball, medal. This format continued unaltered for a number of years. Spacing of play was then as now, alternate Sundays, four before Christmas, four after. If a round was cancelled due to weather it was played on the following Sunday if possible. Seven rounds were usually managed though in the worst year only four were played.

Initially 36 pairs played and in the second year 52. The numbers were kept down at first, players using both tees but later this was changed to a shotgun start to allow more to play. The foursomes has evolved to four fourball events and four foursomes, a few now playing in the afternoon.

The best score ever recorded was a net 60 by Peter Bastow. The worst winning score was a net 79 in torrential rain and wind, with the organisers John and Keith second with an 82! The most extraordinary card was produced by Fred Challis. Starting at the 10th his net score was, 5, 4, 3, 2, 1. The 1 at the 14th was obtained by his holing a wood to the green where Les Yardley, the player in front, was attending the flag for his game.

The picture commemorates the worst ever Winter League morning to that point in time. The entire course was frozen solid with a freezing gale force wind – players were taking as many as ten putts! On this occasion Gordon Marshall took 17 putts, broke his putter across his knee, then remembered he had started at the 10th and still had ten holes to go.

But the popularity of this punishing competition continues unabated. In 1995 there were 144 entrants, all ready to risk the winter weather on the top of the hill!

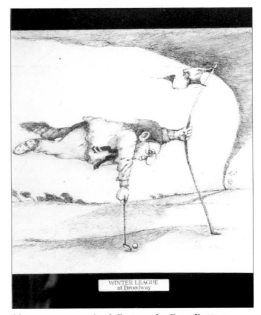

Not an exaggeration! Cartoon by Gary Patterson

1971, Winter League, l to r: K. Gilbert, A. Smith, J. Walker

For many years Aubrey Smith (a member who had always been very generous by providing free printing for the club) presented special mementoes. The winners receive the Gilbert-Walker Cup.

ADMINISTRATION

Up to 1972 with the retirement of Mr. Les Yardley (who at 93 is still playing *and* pulling a trolley) the post of secretary had been an honorary one. With a growing membership it was obvious that there would be too much involved to expect anyone to do the job on a voluntary basis any longer. Mr. E. S. Hart was appointed in 1972 to be followed in 1977 by Mr. Ian Tilbrook for one year only. The gentleman we all remember was Mr. Ken Lawrance who for 12 years administered the club with quiet and determined efficiency until his retirement in February, 1990 when he was made a life member.

As early as 1979 the captain, Mr. Peter Ward was anticipating the need for a full-time manager. By 1990 the affairs of the club certainly needed more than a part-timer and it was decided to engage the services of a full-time managing secretary. Mr. Brian Carnie, a Scot and retired member of the Metropolitan Police, joined the club in this capacity on March 1st, 1990. An EGM was called on August 20th, 1990 to discuss the proposition that now a full-time managing secretary was employed administration could be further streamlined by reducing the size of the committee. After much discussion the proposition was defeated 51 in favour, 80 against.

1990 saw the retirement from office of Mr. Keith Gilbert who for 19 years had been involved in the management of the club as captain, treasurer and president. At the same time Mr. David Senior decided to stand down after 14 years as financial director and treasurer. The position was taken over and competently executed by Mr. Paul Andrews, who will be giving up the job to become captain at the end of 1996.

COMPETITION ORGANISATION

Over the years the club has been fortunate in having found keen and efficient competition secretaries. In 1989 the captain and committee foresaw the value of computer technology in sorting handicaps and competitions and the club is indebted to Mr. Jim Frazer, an ardent computer buff, who was willing to undertake the task of feeding all the necessary information

122

into the computer which they purchased. He remains men's competition secretary as well as sitting on the handicap committee.

A name synonymous with Broadway ladies' competitions is Miss Helen Burton. The ladies of Broadway have been feather-bedded by Helen over many years by having all competition cards marked out for them before commencing play. The notice board in the ladies' room is the envy of many visiting team, the epitome of clarity. On the other side of the coin woe betide any lady who forgets to sign "the book" or fills in the wrong column on her card! In appreciation of her untiring efforts for the ladies' section as well as helping to run mixed competitions, Helen was made an honorary member in 1994.

The computer has now taken over the ladies' handicaps as well as the club's accounts.

THE COURSE

With the completion of the clubhouse, the course has taken on renewed importance. Mr. Cedric Gough has been given the title of course manager, and has been well supported by successive greens committees. All the latest in golf course equipment has been bought so that Broadway must compare well with any club of its type.

A tee improvement project was mooted in July, 1986, and continued through to 1989. Major tee alterations were started by Mr. Mick Webb as chairman of greens and continued by Mr. Tony Holt. Extensive work was done on nine tees. During these years a stone wall repair programme was started, this especially enhanced the approach down to the 5th green and up to the 8th tee as well as marking boundaries right along the 4th fairway.

Cedric Gough 1995

Another new, fully automatic, watering system was installed in 1992 under the greens committee chairmanship of Mr. Arthur Gray. The scheme was to include replacement and increased number of green sprinklers, renewal of water mains system, installation of sprinklers on the tees and one or two vulnerable spots on the fairways, and finally, a second 12,000 gallon reservoir. Total cost of the scheme was £65,000 and a levy of £30 per member was imposed to pay for the work which was completed with a minimum of disruption and now, after only four years, it is impossible to discern where the ground was disturbed. A drinking water supply to the 5th tee was eventually included in the plan.

Modern weedkillers and fertilisers have eliminated buttercups and thistles but in the summer the blossoming clover in the short rough along the 16th puts hundreds of bees in peril! The greens staff are careful to preserve the patches on the course which in spring are covered with cowslips, wild orchids and other flowers which require a botanist's knowledge to describe. However the new captain is a keen conservationist and has plans for Broadway's fauna and flora. The course has its fair share of animals – rabbits (unfortunately), deer, stoats, badgers, snakes. An old hare lived for some years under a fir tree by the side of the 17th fairway and several years ago a stray cat took up residence and accompanied groups of golfers round the course – it even got a mention in *Golf World*.

NINTH PERIOD, 1982–95

1984, EGM April 30th, sale to head greenkeeper of house at South Littleton approved.

1986, EGM September 22nd resolution to build new clubhouse approved, limit £350,000.

1988, EGM August 22nd, extra £80,000 approved to provide fittings for new clubhouse.

1990, Ken Lawrance retires.

1990, first managing secretary, Mr. Brian Carnie, appointed, March 1st.

1990, EGM August 20th, proposals to reduce numbers on committee defeated.

1991, John Freeman, professional, retires – son Martyn takes over as replacement.

1992, new irrigation system, cost £64,000.

1992, 5 day membership discontinued.

Chapter Ten

Centenary Year

A<small>ND</small> so we reach 1995, the hundredth anniversary of the official institution of Broadway Golf Club. The occasion had to be marked and planning was started three years ago with the setting up of a small committee led by the president, Mr. David Robinson.

It was fortuitous that the actual date given by the historian at St. Andrews, April 18th, was Easter Tuesday. This enabled members who would normally be at work to spend their holiday joining in the celebrations. The day was marked by the raising of the Centenary Flag by the oldest and youngest members. The day's golf was a stableford competition, and free buffet with wine was available throughout the day for all members. Fireworks rounded off the occasion. The success of the day augured well for the rest of the year. In fact the club was favoured with the best summer weather there had been for years.

Raising the Centenary Flag 18th April 1995, l to r: L. Arnold, C. Pieters (captain), D. Robinson (president), Christopher O'Hagen

A Centenary Ball was held at Moreton Fire College, which perhaps sounds rather a mundane location, but their facilities are excellent and extensive enough to cater for the expected numbers. Two weeks in the summer were set aside for special Centennial Competitions.

CENTENNIAL PROGRAMME

Friday, June 16th *Centennial Fun Night for Everyone*
(the only chilly day of the fortnight, and unfortunate for the
Caribbean Steel Band playing on the balcony).

Saturday, 17th *Centennial Trophy* – men.
Sunday, 18th *Centennial Greensomes* – mixed.
Monday, 19th *"Geriatrics"* nine hole competition.
Tuesday, 20th *Centennial Trophy* – ladies.
Thursday 22nd *Open team event* – mixed.
Friday, 23rd *Midsummer madness* – mixed.
Saturday, 24th *Centennial AmAm* – mixed.
Sunday, 25th *Centennial Trophy final* – men.
Thursday, 29th *Centennial Trophy* – seniors.
Friday, 30th *Champagne breakfast* – competition
over the "Old Nine Holes".
Saturday, July 1st *Centennial Invitation Day* – men.

Sunday, 2nd *Team Scramble* – mixed
Followed by *Centennial Buffet* and prize giving.

Winners of the Centenary Trophies were:
Men, Gary Betley;
Ladies, Jennifer Foxon;
Juniors, Edward Murray White;
Seniors, Gordon Priddy.

1995 Centenary Trophy Winners, l to r:
J. Foxon, G. Betley, G. Priddy

The club had a successful year in other events. The league team under the captaincy of Tony Hedley had to win their final match to regain their place in the first division. This they did. The ladies league team under the captaincy of Mrs. Sheila Lawson won the first division league for the second year running. In the Gloucester County Team Champi-onships, Broadway's team of Sheila

1995, Ladies League Winners, l to r back row: J. Ward, H. Cooke, L. Chambers, J. Straw, D. Parker, J. Foxon, l to r front row: M. Cave, S. Aitkenhead, S. Lawson (captain), L. Everitt, D. Coleman

Lawson, Sheila Aitkenhead, Diana Chambers and Margaret Riley, won the net prize. 27 teams took part.

One little publicised event brought the captain, Mr. Charles Pieters, "the crowning glory of my year" as he put it. This was the success of the club's quiz team, Brian Wright, Don Palmer, Paul Wragby and Mike Everitt.

1995 Quiz Champions. Back l to r: Sponsers representative, B. Wright, D. Palmer. Front l to r: M. Everitt, P. Wragby

127

After winning regional heats they beat five other clubs from all parts of the country to become UK Club Champions in the final of the Royal Insurance Rules of Golf Quiz at St. Andrews.

The team spent a luxury weekend at the home of golf and won for the club a Toro Greenmaster mower worth over £5,000.

THE FUTURE

At the start of the second hundred years Broadway Golf Club can be in confident mood. In spite of the ups and downs, trials and tribulations of buying and selling property, effects of two world wars the club has excellent facilities, all land and buildings owned by members, with a balance sheet value of £1.25 million.

Playing membership of all kinds stands at 750 plus social members with a waiting list of several years for both men and ladies.

Enthusiasm for the game of golf seems here to stay and fears that commercial clubs which mushroomed after the Ryder Cup successes of the 1980s might be detrimental to private members' clubs have proved unfounded.

The Founder, Dr. Standring would be well satisfied.

Presidents

Note Dates from year elected

1899–1900	I. Averill
1901	Viscount Lifford
1902–10	Lord Elcho
1911–20	T. H. Lloyd
1921–8	Captain F. Burges
1929–32	A. F. de Navarro
1933–45	Dr. W. G. Alexander
1946	Left open
1947–9	C. Rayner-Booth
1950–63	C. H. Gardiner
1964–5	H. O. Roberts
1966–9	G. E. Knight
1970–2	I. F. Tilbrook
1973–4	J. R. Gorin
1975–7	A. W. Harvey
1978–80	F. A. B. Tams
1981–3	M. J. Steward
1984–6	P. Hartwell
1987–9	K. G. Gilbert
1990–2	G. Sloggett
1993–5	D. G. Robinson

Club Captains

Note Dates shown are year of appointment

1922	Dr. C. T. Standring
1923	A. F. de Navarro
1924	Dr. R. E. B. Yelf
1925	Sir Philip Stott
1926	R. B. Harbidge
1927	Dr. J. C. Davies
1928	Dr. W. G. Alexander
1929	A. H. Keyte
1930	G. Pemberton
1931	E. McKillop-Clark
1932	E. McKillop-Clark
1933	Dr. W. G. Alexander
1934	Dr. W. G. Alexander
1935	Dr. W. G. Alexander
1936	Captain W. Ogilvy
1937	Captain W. Ogilvy
1938/46	C. H. Gardiner
1947	R. H. Burlingham
1948	R. H. Burlingham
1949	C. H. Gardiner
1950	G. C. G. Clifford
1951	G. C. G. Clifford
1951	G. C. G. Clifford
1953	C. Pritchard
1954	C. Pritchard
1955	C. Pritchard
1956	G. E. Knight
1957	G. E. Knight
1958	I. F. Tilbrook
1959	I. F. Tilbrook
1960	H. O. Roberts
1961	H. O. Roberts
1962	J. R. Gorin
1963	J. R. Gorin
1964	J. H. Sutton
1965	J. H. Sutton
1966	A. W. Harvey
1967	L. A. Reynolds
1968	A. G. Chandler
1969	R. L. Denison
1970	C. G. Price
1971	M. J. Steward
1972	F. A. B. Tams OBE
1973	W. C. Short
1974	J. S. Walker
1975	K. G. Gilbert
1976	Dr. W. M. Savery
1977	G. Sloggett
1978	P. Hartwell
1979	P. W. Ward
1980	D. G. Robinson
1981	D. S. Palmer
1982	D. H. Senior
1983	A. J. Gardner
1984	A. E. Powers
1985	J. M. Webb
1986	S. E. Clews
1987	G. A. Grey
1988	A. T. Godfrey
1989	F. Penny
1990	R. C. D. Cumper
1991	S. Linley
1992	D. H. Evans
1993	R. D. Matthews
1994	G. J. Bate
1995	C. Pieters

Lady Captains

1955–6	Miss J. C. Hoskins
1957–8	Mrs. K. Stockdale
1959–60	Miss B. Stanley
1961–2	Mrs. M. Roberts
1963–4	Mrs. K. A. Jennings
1965	Mrs. K. Stockdale
1966	Miss J. M. Foxon
1967	Mrs. A. M. Mason
1968	Mrs. E. E. Feaver
1969	Miss J. C. Hoskins
1979	Mrs. R. G. Haydon
1971	Mrs. A. Short
1972	Mrs. J. E. Armstrong
1973	Mrs. F. I. L. Cooke
1974	Mrs. P. J. Morgan
1975	Mrs. A. M. Booth
1976	Mrs. E. K. Harrison
1977	Mrs. G. A. Challis
1978	Mrs. E. J. Walker
1979	Mrs. W. A. Thorpe
1980	Mrs. D. M. Tilbrook
1981	Miss M. Caudwell
1982	Mrs. S. M. Stacey
1983	Mrs. P. F. Chapman
1984	Mrs. M. L. Cave
1985	Mrs. B. Palmer
1986	Mrs. A. Denison
1987	Mrs. M. Valler
1988	Mrs. P. E. Young
1989	Mrs. J. Straw
1990	Mrs. V. Linley
1991	Mrs. E. Marshall
1992	Mrs. D. Hill
1993	Mrs. C. A. Matthews
1994	Mrs. G. E. Dunsby
1995	Mrs. D. Coleman

Honorary Secretaries

Dr. C. T. Standring
  April 1895 to 15.10.1921
Dr. W. G. Alexander
  15.10.1921 to 19.11.1932
C. Rayner Booth
  29.10.1932 to 2.5.1956

W. B. Dalrynple MC
  2.5.1956 to 15.1.1964
H. W. E. Butcher
  15.1. 1964 to 14.12.1966
H. W. Mason
  14.12.1966 to 20.10.1969

L. T. Yardley 20. 10. 1969 to
  16.10.1972

Secretaries

E. S. Hart
  16.10.1972 to 31.1.1977

I. F. Tilbrook
  1.2.1977 to 31.3.1978

K. S. Lawrance
  1.4.1978 to 28.2.1990

Managing Secretaries
B. Carnie 1.3.1990 to

Professionals

C. Mayo 1903
Frank Bisgrove 1923-63

John Freeman 1963-1991

Martyn Freeman 1991

Life Members

1922	A. J. Balfour	1967	R. J. Barker	1987	R. Hancock
1924	Dr. C. T. Standring	1967	H. W. E. Butcher	1988	L. E. T. Arnold
1929	J. H. Jones	1967	C. Pritchard	1989	K. S. Lawrance
1932	Dr. W. G. Alexander	1969	H. W. Mason	1991	J. Gorin
1936	A. H. Keyte	1972	L. T. Yardley	1991	J. W. Freeman
1954	H. T. Ogden	1973	H. G. Lamb	1992	Mrs. K. Jennings
1954	R. A. Eaton	1977	F. I. W. Gash	1993	H. Cook
1964	F. Bisgrove	1978	Mrs. M. Roberts	1994	Miss H. L. Burton
1964	C. H. Gardiner	1980	I. F. Tilbrook		
1964	W. D. Dalrymple	1985	F. A. B. Tams OBE		

Club Champions

1965	A. G. Chandler	1976	M. H. Lee	1987	M. P. Humpston
1966	T. R. Gorin	1977	M. H. Lee	1988	M. P. Humpston
1967	T. R. Gorin	1978	F. Powers	1989	M. Dove
1968	T. R. Gorin	1979	D. L. Singer	1990	M. Dove
1969	A. G. Chandler	1980	D. L. Singer	1991	M. Dove
1970	T. R. Gorin	1981	T. R. Gorin	1992	J. Webber
1971	T. R. Gorin	1982	D. M. Fletcher	1993	S. R. Thornhill
1972	A. G. Chandler	1983	D. M. Fletcher	1994	S. Griffin
1973	T. R. Gorin	1984	F. Powers	1995	M. P. Humpston
1974	T. R. Gorin	1985	D. M. Fletcher		
1975	T. R. Gorin	1986	M. P. Humpston		

Lady Champions

1982	J. M. Foxon	1987	J. M. Foxon	1992	J. M. Foxon
1983	J. M. Foxon	1988	H. V. Cooke	1993	J. M. Foxon
1984	J. M. Foxon	1989	H. V. Cooke	1994	L. Chambers
1985	J. M. Foxon	1990	H. V. Cooke	1995	L. Chambers
1986	S. G. Aitkenhead	1991	J. M. Foxon